# A HIGHER CALLING

# A HIGHER CALLING

Pursuing Love, Faith,
and Mount Everest
for a Greater Purpose

## CAPTAIN HAROLD
### *and*
## RACHEL EARLS

WATERBROOK

UNCORRECTED PROOF

SPECIAL SALES

Most WaterBrook books are available at special quantity discounts when purchased in bulk by corporations, organizations, and special-interest groups. Custom imprinting or excerpting can also be done to fit special needs. For information, please email

specialmarketscms@penguinrandomhouse.com.

# Contents

# Prologue

*My husband might die.*

I'm wide awake, lying on my back, staring at the ceiling in an unfamiliar room, while these four words loop in my head. I am staying with a friend and fellow military wife in Colorado. Earlier in the day, I tried to keep my composure. But now, in the quiet darkness, I can't hold back my tears. The worry has set in strong, as this possibility feels very real. Much too real.

*Harold might die.*

My husband, my best friend and the love of my life, chose to leave me to climb a massive mountain halfway across the world . . . and he wasn't even a climber when I met him three years ago!

We haven't been married for a full year yet. I decided I couldn't sit at home waiting for Harold. I wanted my own story and my own adventure. I needed a change of pace if I was going to keep my sanity. I didn't want to stop living a full life and feel stuck in a period of waiting. My plan was to make the most of our time apart, so I embarked on my own trip, leaving Georgia and flying to Colorado, with plans to continue on to several other spots.

Harold had called me a few hours earlier from Mount Everest's Advanced Base Camp. He'd sounded exhausted as he told me about the significant snowstorm headed his way, forcing his team to climb back down to a lower elevation. I know with bad weather conditions, a tired body, and many hours of descending in low visibility, the chances of something going wrong are significantly higher.

I was feeling okay until I received an email from Tommy, Harold's best friend and their team's camp manager. I open it again, noting the parts that stand out.

> I woke up this morning to a snowstorm at Base Camp. . . .
>
> I do not know how extreme this snowstorm is up there but can imagine it has been significant. . . .
>
> They are currently snowed in at ABC. . . .
>
> The snow will delay any movement for several days. . . .
>
> The trails are currently under snow and avalanches will be more prevalent with the fresh powder. . . .
>
> Please pray that the weather clears up for our team and the others at higher camps and that everybody makes smart decisions, as I expect they will. . . .

Tommy's email says movement is delayed, yet I know they are pressing on. Is my husband making a bad decision—perhaps a fatal one?

I'm terrified. I don't know when I'll hear from him next, if at all.

I am trying to be strong. To enjoy my own adventures. But deep down, I'm afraid of being left alone. I fear if something does happen, I will blame Harold for making the choice to leave. Or maybe I'll blame myself for letting him go.

These aren't the typical worries of a twenty-four-year-old newlywed, but they are my reality until Harold is finally home and in my arms. Every day I'm realizing how precious and fragile life is and what truly matters. It's not the material things, the success, the money, or our physical appearances. It's the people we love.

*The little moments count.*

Living with that truth in the forefront of your mind changes you. It's changing me. I am starting to approach life with an attitude of thanksgiving, even in the midst of my trials. I realize my time with Harold is limited, and time is better spent being joyful and living in love than living in anger, frustration, or stress. I remind myself something I have told others: *You are capable of more than you can imagine. And with God by your side, you will always come out stronger!*

It would be easy to let fear take over, but I'm not going to allow fear to write my story. I won't be controlled by my current circumstances. Tonight, I choose faith over fear. Just like I did this morning. Just like I will do again tomorrow and the next day and the next. Until Harold is back with me and we are facing our next adventure together.

As I lie in bed, wiping the tears off my cheeks, I think about all those moments early in our relationship, and I realize something. Little moments can turn out to be big moments, the life-changing ones. Like being contacted out of the blue by a stranger who turns out to be the love of your life . . .

# A HIGHER CALLING

# The First Message

**HAROLD**

Spoiler alert! I didn't choose the princess. This love story is a bit more unconventional. In this tale, the guy meets the gal, falls in love, and instead of conquering the dragon, takes off to conquer the world's tallest mountain, leaving her to question if there will even be a happily ever after.

For my entire childhood, I was dead certain I would meet a girl and it would be love at first sight. No question about it. I was sure God had a grand, crazy plan for the way I was going to meet my wife.

I grew up knowing what I wanted out of life and never being scared to go after it. Wild adventures filled my bucket list, from visiting the Maasai tribe on the plains of Africa to exploring the Amazon Rainforest. However, climbing Mount Everest topped the list.

I don't hold back from dreaming big, and once I have a dream in mind, I can't stop thinking about it until I make it happen. If I say I'm going to do something, I will do it or literally die trying. I can't say that's the healthiest way to live, especially if the dream is deadly and means leaving behind the ones you love, but that's who I am.

I had just started my sophomore year at the United States Military Academy at West Point. I was playing baseball and was part of the Corps of Cadets.

One weekend I was able to get away and meet my best friend, Tommy, at Disney World. It wasn't long before I made eye contact with a very pretty girl. She had long hair and attracted quite a crowd. Kids flocked around her, staring as they waited in line to talk to her. She was none other than Princess Jasmine.

As Tommy and I passed, she looked straight at me in her turquoise two-piece and waved. Or maybe she was motioning for the little kids to walk around us. Either way, I immediately got butterflies.

*Maybe she's the one*, I thought.

After she was done signing all the kids' booklets and foreheads, she walked up to us and smiled. "Are you boys too nervous to talk to a princess?"

I fainted. No, not really, but I felt like I could have. Jasmine must cast spells in addition to granting wishes, because I was hooked! I finally got my nerve up, chased her down, and asked her on a date. *Take that, Aladdin!* Maybe it was a little cocky of me to think God had set aside a literal princess for me, but nothing is too big for God!

After my date with Princess Jasmine, though, I realized there wasn't much there besides an initial physical attraction. I knew the type of relationship I wanted would require a deeper emotional connection and a foundation rooted in God. I imagine God chuckles at us when we think we have it all figured out according to our own master plans, when what we really need to do is loosen our grip on being in control and see what He has in store for us.

Little did I know, God had someone for me who far exceeded any princess I could have dreamed of. Instead, she was an everyday, sweatpants-wearing, brownie-loving, strong, independent, God-fearing woman. She didn't wear makeup often, she rarely woke up before nine in the morning, and her car was usually missing a hubcap. But, man, did I fall head over heels for her . . . and fast.

## RACHEL

Let's all take a moment to laugh at the fact that Harold thought Princess Jasmine is the one who grants wishes. The genie would be so offended! That's my husband for you: master of mixing up story lines and butchering song lyrics. I can't say those were qualities I was looking for in a spouse, but I've come to love his quirks.

When I began looking for a partner in life, it was important to me to find someone who was ambitious and passionate about working toward his goals, and, boy, did I find him. I met a man who believed big dreams were possible and chased them down with everything he had. This relentless drive, a quality that made me fall in love with him, would also lead him to pursue a dangerous dream that placed both of us on a precarious journey. A journey that easily might have killed Harold.

Like most girls, I have always loved love. Chick flicks are my jam, and I often dreamed about how my own love story would play out. I wanted a love better than what was in books and television shows, better than anything I could imagine. I'm not going to lie, though; I didn't know if that kind of great love actually existed in the real world.

By the time I was a sophomore in college, I was discouraged by the thought of love. Actually, *discouraged* doesn't do justice to the intensity of my feelings. I felt broken, confused, angry, and lost. I had all but stopped believing in love. I had just ended a relationship with someone I thought I saw my future with, and I had never felt that kind of heartache before. It was a deep ache in my soul that wouldn't go away. It lingered and festered. Truthfully, I listened to some of the lies it created in my head. I allowed questions to consume me until I was drowning in self-doubt.

It's natural to hold on to things for too long, but healing can't happen until we finally let go. I was hurt, and I didn't want to be hurt again. I built walls, became closed off, and pushed away interested guys for a time. I still longed to be loved and to give love in return, but I didn't feel like it would ever happen for me. Quite frankly, I had a lot of healing to do.

I spent the next year working on my heart and grew to be content being single. I did, however, continue to pray for my future husband, even though I was pretty sure I wouldn't meet him until I was out of college. In my mind, I knew everyone I was going to know in college already, and there was no way any of them were the man God intended for me.

Turns out God had a different plan.

One night before bed, at the start of my junior year, I wrote this in my journal:

*Hey, God,*

*Thank You for loving me unconditionally and pursuing me relentlessly. My heart is happy, and You know it's been a long road of healing. I trust in Your plan for my life and I know in Your timing, You'll bring the right man into my life. I don't need that right now, and it's okay if it's much further down the road than I thought. But can You just give me a sign that he is out there?*

*I love You so much, and I'm excited for what this year has to bring. I'm ready!*

*Love, Rach*

The very next day I got a strange Facebook message from a guy I'd never heard of. His name was Harold.

## HAROLD

For over a year, Tommy had been telling me about his redheaded cousin.

"You have to meet her," Tommy said. "Her name's Rachel, and she's awesome."

"Sorry, man. I'm just not that into redheads."

No offense to all the beautiful redheads out there. I was clearly delusional.

Eventually he showed me a picture of Rachel. Hot diggity dog! My jaw dropped. I didn't expect her to be a knockout, given Tommy's looks. (It's fun taking jabs at your best friend when you're writing a book!) To be honest, Tommy is a good-looking dude. I should have known that Rachel would probably share the family's good looks.

"Why didn't you show me her picture before?" I asked.

"I tried, but I got you now," Tommy told me. "I'll put in a good word for you. I'm sure she already knows who you are."

The fact that Tommy spoke so highly of Rachel said a lot. He knew both of us and understood what I wanted most in life: a family. He told me Rachel would make an incredible mother and described her tender and nurturing spirit. When he vouched for her character and spoke of the way she loved the Lord, I was more blown away than when I first saw her gorgeous photograph. Yes, Rachel was a total knockout, but there was so much more that drew me to her. It seemed our characters, values, and goals we were chasing in life were aligned.

A couple of months later, Tommy made it sound like he had talked to Rachel and smoothed the way for me to message her. Certain he'd made her aware of me, I decided to send her a Facebook message. I worked hard to write a message that would have just the right tone: friendly, confident, funny, and not too desperate.

**Harold Earls IV**
Sep 13, 2012

Rachel, from what I hear you are a pretty awesome girl! So, I figured I'd boldly and lamely introduce myself to you over Facebook. I am currently in a relationship with your cousin Tommy and he is always talking you up,

so I figured I should definitely look to meet this girl he
speaks so highly of.

In hindsight, it was a really lame message. But I was trying to
be funny!

**RACHEL**

I had no idea who Harold Earls IV was. My cousin Tommy hadn't
mentioned anything to me. In fact, I just assumed this Harold guy
might be another distant cousin of mine I didn't know. Our only
mutual friends on Facebook were my family members (I have a
pretty big extended family).

I had always thought highly of my cousin Tommy—he's the
kind of guy who makes you a better person just by being around
him. I knew if Harold was his best friend, Harold had to be a solid
guy.

I was a little intrigued by the odd yet endearing message. So,
what did I do? I called my mom, the knower-of-all-things-family-
and-drama. "Mom! What's going on here? Who is this Harold guy?
And what kind of weird name is Harold?"

"I have no idea," she replied.

"I don't believe you." It was too bizarre for her not to know
something. But I'll give it to her—she was pretty convincing.

"I really don't know!" she insisted.

I decided to text Tommy's mom, Meredith, to inquire further
about this handsome man messaging me, and, boy, did she take that
as an opportunity to sing Harold's praises. She told me that he came
from a strong Christian family, had a good head on his shoulders,
and had a zest for life like I did and that she genuinely felt we would
make a good team. Coming from someone I looked up to, this af-
firmation carried a lot of weight.

I decided this Harold guy might be worth my time and shot him
a quick message back.

**Rachel Wynn: Sep 13, 2012**
Bet good ole Tommy makes a great boyfriend! I love
Tommy!

## HAROLD

My friend Tommy is a good and godly man. We've known each
other since high school, and the two of us have encouraged each
other, read the Bible together, and attended church together. We
have repeated to each other the popular Andy Stanley quote "Start
becoming the person the person you're looking for is looking for."*

We watched romantic comedies like we were studying game
film: "Tommy, did you see that? He went 90 percent of the way for
the kiss, and then she went the final 10 percent. Write that down."

When Rachel messaged me back, I was thankful Tommy had
reached out to her ahead of time (or so I thought). I assumed my
joke introduction had been a big success. We continued messaging
each other. I spent tons of time, sometimes an hour or two, crafting
my messages in Microsoft Word, then copying and pasting the note
into Facebook. I wanted to come up with the most clever responses,
and that took time. Frankly, she was way out of my league and a
grade above me in college, and I was nervous I would screw it up!

I was afraid she wasn't into me, because her responses were
quick, with little or no flirty emojis. I worked to become a man
worthy of her while pursuing her intentionally. It makes me think
of some wisdom from my pastor, Ben Stuart: "If you're pursuing
someone, be clear about your intentions. If you're interested in getting to know her for the purpose of it leading to a relationship, let
her know. If you aren't interested, let her know. Being clear about
your intentions will take the stress out of trying to figure out where
you stand with each other."

---

* Andy Stanley, *The New Rules for Love, Sex, and Dating* (Grand Rapids, MI:
Zondervan, 2014), 192.

I proceeded with this strategy for a couple of days, logging in to Facebook to copy and paste my message, then quickly signing off. Until one day everything changed. I logged in to send her a message, and before I could log off again, she messaged me back. *Oh shoot!* I thought. I had to come up with a response right then.

My cursor was blinking, and so, too, were the three dots letting her know I was on and responding. I panicked. Like sweaty hands, clammy face, and hives kind of panic. Okay, maybe not the hives part, but it was intense. The pressure was on, and I was forced to engage in an actual back-and-forth conversation.

To my surprise, it went well. But then Tommy logged on to my Facebook account from his computer without my knowing and started sending fake messages to Rachel right in the middle of our conversation! Once I realized what was going on (I could hear Tommy laughing in my head), I asked Rachel for her phone number so I could text her and hopefully salvage the rest of our conversation.

Lesson learned: don't give your best friend your Facebook login.

I spent the next several days texting her between my classes, baseball, and studying. I'd get this big goofy grin on my face every time I saw Rachel's name pop up on my phone, excited to see what new question she had or to read her heartfelt responses. There was so much depth to our conversations, which made the distance between us seem insignificant.

She was in college in Florida, while I was in college in New York. We learned that depth overcomes distance. The more I learned about Rachel, the more it became clear that we were equally yoked. For example, we both valued new experiences in the world more than worldly possessions. I had never met someone whose approach to life seemed to align so well with my own.

What have I gotten myself into?

I stand at an elevation of twelve thousand feet in Lhasa, China, during our ten-day excursion across the Tibetan Plateau, and I see the mountain for the first time. It's not the beautiful, graceful, white-frosted peak of my fairy-tale daydreams, with fluffy little dandelions in the valley. This Everest is darker, almost black, without much snow. It appears wild, intense, and wicked. The journey ahead of me is huge, super steep, and absolutely terrifying. Chills run through me.

This is no joke.

I see a cloud at the top, formed off the back side of the peak, but then quickly realize I am actually looking at the jet stream angrily ripping snow and ice off the summit. Where I stand, the day is perfectly sunny, but over there, the mountain exhibits deadly conditions. All the statistics I've read about the dangers, the widowed wives, and the extreme elements begin to cycle through my mind. I think of the frozen bodies on the mountain, all those brave souls who never made it back down. Then I think of Rachel at home alone.

Internally, I'm panicking, but outwardly, I'm celebrating our first glance of the mountain with the rest of the team. "Nice, there's Everest!" I say as high fives are shared. Deep inside, however, I can't help but think about the very real possibility of dying on that steep, dark mountain.

# Love at First Phone Call

*Sunday, September 23, 2012*

**RACHEL**

Ten days after his first Facebook message, Harold called me out of the blue. It was 8:07 p.m. on a Sunday, and I was walking to my car to meet some friends for dinner when my phone started vibrating. My initial thought? *It's probably my mom calling for the umpteenth time today.*

Boy, was I caught off guard when I saw Harold's name pop up. A big smile spread across my face as my excitement level shot sky high. At the same time, my body was riddled with nerves. This would be the first time we actually spoke; I realized I'd never heard his voice before.

I picked up the call as I climbed into my car. I drove to the restaurant while we talked, but I never went inside. I didn't want our conversation to end, so I sat in the parking lot with my feet propped on the dash and my seat reclined, talking to Harold as the night sky grew darker and darker. After an hour or two, I drove home and parked again, still talking. Finally, I went up to my room, and we talked until 2:07 a.m.

We talked for six hours straight about our families, our goals, God, our pasts, the present, and the future. He was really open about the way God had shaped him over the years. It was refreshing to hear a man speak with so much honesty and vulnerability about his past and what he wanted in the future. He wasn't holding back, and he wasn't sugarcoating anything. We were simply two people sharing our hearts and discovering that we were running in the same direction. I felt like my heart, which I had previously closed, was opening back up to this person I'd never even met. Whatever was going on between us was very different from anything I'd ever known before or expected.

It sounds insane to say, but I knew from that first call that he was my person. It happened fast, yet it was so clear to me. Though our relationship did develop quickly, I don't want to give the illusion that it randomly fell into place for us. We had worked on ourselves individually so we would both be in the right place with God and be the best versions of ourselves before we pursued a relationship together.

## HAROLD

It was a cool September evening when I called Rachel from under the lights on the baseball field at West Point. As we talked, I walked barefoot around the field until my feet felt frozen, at which point I decided to head back to my barracks room. I crawled into my top bunk as I continued talking with Rachel, whispering so I wouldn't wake my roommate.

I can remember saying, "Rachel, you are it. I found you." I lay there and stared at the wall in a daze. Suddenly, everything was different. I had never felt the way I did during our phone call. It was the most intimate conversation I'd ever had with a person, let alone someone I technically had not even met.

*How was this even possible?*

But it was. From that first conversation, I was done. The attraction I felt when I saw her beautiful picture was still there. Yet as I got to know her heart, how she was chasing God and what passions were ignited within her, it was obvious we were on the same page in life, and that was truly a more beautiful thing.

## RACHEL

People talk about love at first sight, and not everyone believes it can happen. But for us, it was love at first phone call. I imagine if we'd spent six hours together in person, I would have been distracted thinking about if or when he would hold my hand or kiss me. Instead, that call allowed us to dig deeper and not be distracted by physical attraction. While physical intimacy is vital in marriage, most of marriage is actually living life together, so it's healthy to find someone who you can talk to forever and never get bored with.

After that first phone call, Harold and I talked on the phone or video chatted for hours each night. I'd get off the phone and my cheeks would be sore from smiling the entire time. There was this excitement stirring in my heart that radiated out of me. I wanted to tell everyone about him! In fact, I used to stand in my sorority dinner line waiting with my friends and pull up his Facebook pictures to show to them.

Although my heart had previously been broken and I questioned ever finding love, I had spent the year healing, and that little girl in me, dreaming of a fairy tale, was hopeful this crazy story beginning to unfold would be the answer to my prayers. The breakup I'd gone through helped me realize that if the person I thought was so great wasn't the right person for me, it meant God had someone even better for me. I made a promise with myself and God that settling in a relationship was not an option. I was determined to find someone who would always fight for me and never make me question my worth. God led me to Harold.

Harold wasn't perfect, and I didn't expect him to be, but I never felt I would be settling if I ended up with him. It was quite the opposite, actually; I could see myself growing and becoming a better person because of him. We prayed together during our video chats, and whenever I was stressed about school or started feeling down, he would refocus my attention on God and help me see the bigger picture. He encouraged me not to hold back when it came to my dreams and pushed me to believe in myself and reach my full potential.

One of the qualities that stood out to me about Harold was how he continually worked on self-development and pushed himself to learn new things. I'm not just talking about studying what he learned in school. He would research how to be a better communicator, learn tricks for remembering people's names, expand his vocabulary, and so on. I loved how he was always working to improve himself and wasn't complacent; it showed me that with time, he would only become a better partner as he kept pushing himself to grow as a person.

Harold was an absolute superhero for staying up all night talking to me and then waking up a few short hours later for his morning military formation. Sometimes, though, he'd fall asleep during our calls (I mean hard-core sleeping, the kind where he'd start snoring and drooling!) and I'd get offended. It didn't feel good to pour out my heart and notice I was literally putting him to sleep. I mean, I know I'm not that boring! I had to learn not to take it personally and to understand that at West Point, the responsibilities and schoolwork are endless. This meant the time he was spending talking to me was time he didn't freely have. He was sacrificing sleep in order to make me a priority, and that more than made up for the few times I'd catch him with his eyes closed midconversation.

At this point, we still hadn't met in person, although it felt like we had known each other our entire lives. I invited him to be my date at a sorority function in November, and he happily accepted.

I had butterflies even thinking about what it would be like when we met face to face. Little did I know, he had secretly been making plans to surprise me with a visit in October, a whole month earlier.

As a decoy, my friend Morgan invited me to a beach weekend with her family, so I packed my swimsuits and shorts and went to her apartment the night before we were planning to leave. Earlier, I had sent Harold pictures of my swimsuits and asked him to help me pick which ones to bring. He must have been grinning at how clueless I was.

Morgan and I were hanging out in the living room, watching *Friends* in our pajamas, which for me meant Nike running shorts, a super baggy camo T-shirt, and no makeup. Our friend Lauren was on her way over so she could introduce us to a guy she had met. They were both in on Harold's surprise too!

A little after midnight, Harold called. Just a few seconds into our phone call, Lauren and her guy (who is now her husband) walked in the door. I politely told Harold I would call him back. He started acting weird, like he didn't want me to hang up. I didn't want to be rude to my friend, so I told him again that I'd call back later. That's when he said, "Why would you call me back when I'm already here?" *And he walked through the door!*

I was in complete shock! He was wearing a blue collared button-up shirt with khaki pants and a belt, and there I was looking like I just got back from a duck hunt in my oversize camo shirt. It wasn't exactly how I pictured he'd see me for the first time. Had I even showered? How bad did my armpits stink? What on earth had my friends been thinking? A heads-up would have been nice, but to be honest, I was so overcome with excitement that I immediately jumped to my feet and hugged him.

In that moment, none of those things mattered to either of us. My entire body was shaking, and I couldn't seem to get any words out other than "What? What?" I couldn't connect the dots. I didn't understand what was going on because in my mind, my friends and

I were supposed to be going to the beach. And, last I knew, Harold was in New York City having a night with his guys.

Harold is convinced I cried, but I didn't. I was way too confused to cry. But oh, buddy, was I full of joy! I'd never been that happy to see anyone before. It was like a movie scene you want to replay over and over. That was the defining moment that confirmed everything I was already feeling. I really had found my person, and I'd take that over a beach trip any day!

Harold and I headed over to Lauren's apartment and hung out in the living room all night, with no intention of sleeping. We basically talked each other's ears off until sunrise.

At one point, Harold looked at me and said, "You're my girlfriend."

"I am?" I responded, slightly confused about how I had missed the moment when that happened but also jumping up and down and throwing a party in my head.

"Wait, do you wanna be?" he said with the cutest mixture of uncertainty and excitement.

My answer was easy. "Yes!"

## HAROLD

She was definitely crying when we first met. At least, I remember it that way. One thing I know for certain is my heart was racing about three hundred beats a minute. When I saw Rachel in person, I'm not kidding, she was the most beautiful woman I'd ever laid eyes on. That was the sexiest men's extra-large camo T-shirt I'd ever seen! I couldn't get any words out; all I could do was smile. We wrapped our arms around each other, and I wanted to never let go. I was doing my best to freeze that moment in time. It was the best first hug of my life.

I was so nervous leading up to that moment. Not because I didn't know if we would actually have a connection but in anticipation for what that moment meant. From our first phone call, I knew she was the one, so you can imagine the intense feelings building up as I made my way to meet my future wife for the first time. I felt such a deep emotional and physical attraction to her, a connection I had never experienced with anyone else. I felt she fully understood me. My past, my passions, what made me tick, what I cared about, where I was headed, and what I wanted to be—she accepted all of me.

Our excitement made us forget how tired we were. We must have fallen asleep at exactly the same time, and when we woke up, intertwined like a pretzel, our eyes were just inches apart. It was like one of those Hollywood rom-coms, where the guy and girl wake up and gaze into each other's eyes, smiling warmly as the sunlight hits their faces. That actually happened, except I'm not sure Rachel thought it was as romantic as I did.

"Oh my gosh," Rachel said. "I smell gross. The sun is blinding me, and I need to shower and brush my teeth."

I heard my stomach gurgling. "I'm starving."

We had forgotten to eat. We had only eighteen hours before I had to be back on campus at West Point, which meant we had just a few hours left together. We ended up grabbing some food before heading to the airport. When I picked up the tab and signed the receipt, I wrote, "Harold Earls likes Rachel Wynn." Even though the waiter must have been confused and probably made fun of how cheesy I was, I didn't care. I knew it would make Rachel smile.

At the airport, I got Rachel a gate pass so she could wait with me until the very last boarding call. We were kissing and hugging, the ultimate annoying lovebirds who literally can't keep their hands off each other. I heard someone ask, "Y'all just get engaged?"

"Pretty much," I said.

## RACHEL

That's a pretty gutsy response after spending not even a full twenty-four hours with a girl, but earlier he'd made an even gutsier move. I have a little diamond ring my grandmother gave me that I wore on my right hand. A couple of hours earlier, Harold switched it over to my ring finger on my left hand.

"I like the way that looks," he told me.

Perhaps it was because it looked like I was wearing an engagement ring, or maybe it was the way in which Harold was affectionately gazing at me that drew the comment from the stranger. Either way, the remark made us smile. It affirmed the strength of our connection in a very powerful way.

After Harold left, I took a screenshot of the time and date he'd called me just before he walked in to surprise me. I knew in my heart this was a pivotal moment in my life, so I wanted to document everything.

*My life is about to change*, I thought. *He's military and he plays baseball.* Neither was overly appealing to me, but I did enjoy seeing Harold in both uniforms. I fully appreciated and had the utmost respect for our military, but it wasn't necessarily the life I wanted for my own family. I knew I was in this relationship for the long haul, so I was facing the reality that it would require a lot of sacrifice on my end.

It's impossible to have commitment without sacrifice; both are required in a strong relationship. Sometimes the sacrifices are small, and sometimes they are life altering. I knew this was going to be a life-altering sacrifice, but I also knew that what I was gaining was much greater. I wanted a life with Harold, which meant any sacrifice would be worth it.

Never in my wildest dreams could I have imagined the kinds of sacrifices a life together would mean for us.

Though I can't see the mountain in the dark of night on the Tibetan Plateau, I still feel it shadowing over me in the distance. I downplay my fears and nerves when I talk with Rachel. I tell her things like "It's not too scary" and "It's really pretty" and "I'm not too worried about it." These are half truths. In reality, this towering beast in the background is the meanest, blackest thing I've ever seen. I'm worried, and I'm humbled. I could share this with her, my best friend and biggest supporter. But I want to protect her from the knot in my stomach, the nerves constantly rumbling inside, and the nagging questions: What am I doing? and What have I left behind?

Have you ever come to a point in your life when the one thing you've been working toward suddenly seems insurmountable? A moment when your own personal Everest (be it creating a business, parenting, etc.) stares you down, looking bigger and scarier than you ever could have imagined? A time when you feel intimidated and alone? A time in which you suddenly begin to question everything? That's what I'm doing in China, asking over and over again, Have I bitten off more than I can chew? I know life sometimes presents moments that feel impossible. But I also know when you overcome these challenges, you come out stronger. I just hope I'm up to the task.

As we continue our trek to Everest's Base Camp, the mountain looms in the distance, growing larger with every step I take.

# "We're All a Little Weird. And Life Is a Little Weird."

**RACHEL**

It was 3:15 a.m., and we'd just finished video chatting. When I got in bed, I grabbed my journal off my nightstand and wrote two notes, the first one to God and the second one to Harold.

*Hey, God!*

*Gosh, You are working in my life in some crazy ways. First, I want to stop and thank You. Thank You for loving me as Your child! I am in love with You, and now I have found a man whose heart matches Yours. God, tonight I realized that I love him! I want to make sure we always keep You at the center of our relationship. God, I pray that You guide him in his decision-making and align his goals and aspirations with Your plan for his life! May Your will be done in our relationship, and may we follow You, growing closer together as we fall more and more in love with You. I love You so much, God, it fills my heart with joy. Help me find more ways to serve You and listen to You easier!*

*So in love, Rach*

*Dear Harold,*

*Tonight, I realized that I am in love with you! The first night of Beach Retreat when we were talking on the phone about the future, my heart was overwhelmed, and to be honest, I was a little scared. Then on Oct 18 @ 1:11, I wrote down in my phone that I loved you, two days before I even met you in person, but still I was scared to admit it because it was all so fast! That night I felt all kinds of emotions, and I knew I never wanted to let you go! Tonight, I am not doubting anymore; it may not have been a moment we were physically together, but it was the moment I fell in love with your heart! There are so many things I love about you, but I realized that I love you because I love who God is in you. I feel closer to God and more in love with Him when I am with you. This is the kind of love that I want. This is real. Harold, I love you! I want to spend the rest of our lives together falling more in love with each other as we fall more in love with God. Forever and always.*

*Love, Rach*

This verse was printed at the bottom of my journal page: "Every good gift and every perfect gift is from above, and comes down from the Father" (James 1:17). It made me smile as I read it, knowing that Harold and our love were gifts from God.

During the Thanksgiving holiday, a month after Harold moved my grandmother's ring to my left ring finger, he met my parents for the first time. He walked straight up to my mother, who is five foot eleven, and said, "Wow, you really are tall. That's good genes for our kids." He's a bold one all right, and he wasn't shy about how he felt about me!

We were at my family's cabin in North Carolina, and I decided to tell Harold I loved him that night by reading him the letter I'd written in my journal. I'd been waiting for this moment. As I began to read what I wrote, my eyes welled up with tears that dripped onto the page. My voice shook with emotion. As soon as Harold realized what I was doing, he interrupted me and told me that he loved me. He put his arms around me and pulled me in close, and we both cried happy tears.

To this day, we still debate over who said it first. One time Harold told me he loved me during a video chat, but he said it in Arabic, so it didn't really count. I usually win the debate in the end, since I was the first one to say it in English. I'd used Google Translate to figure out what he said, though, so I knew he was feeling the same way. He had told me he had made a vow that he was only going to say "I love you" to the person he was planning to marry, and I knew he had never said those three words to anyone else before.

## HAROLD

There were so many little things that made me fall in love with Rachel. Like the way she said my name, the cute freckle on her lip, her utter lack of a sense of direction, and her contagious smile. The greatest feeling was being able to act super silly around each other. We could be ourselves and know we wouldn't judge but only love each other more for our weirdness. In his book *True Love*, Robert Fulghum said, "We're all a little weird. And life is a little weird. And when we find someone whose weirdness is compatible with ours, we join up with them and fall into mutually satisfying weirdness—and call it love."* This is the perfect way to describe our relationship, and I wouldn't have it any other way!

Unfortunately, during the first month Rachel and I were officially dating, my parents announced they were getting a divorce. I had an amazing childhood growing up, with a loving father and

* Robert Fulghum, *True Love: Stories Told to and by Robert Fulghum* (New York: HarperCollins, 1997), 115.

mother and a younger sister, but this traumatic event left me not knowing what a good marriage looked like. I spent a lot of time processing, questioning, and reflecting with Rachel. Seeing my family crumble left a lasting impression on me, and it strengthened my commitment to Rachel. We pledged to put each other first always. I'd seen firsthand how my parents placed their kids and work before their marriage, and though they were the greatest parents on earth, they sacrificed their marriage in the process of raising their family.

I remember Tommy's mom, Meredith, telling Rachel and me that the greatest gift a couple can give their kids is to show them what a loving relationship looks like. A loving relationship is making time for each other, holding hands, and kissing in public. It's telling and showing Rachel how much I love her. It's love-tapping Rachel's bum when she is cooking in the kitchen. It's slow dancing in the living room after a hard day. It's smearing brownie batter on her face and chasing her around the house, giggling.

A loving relationship is also apologizing when we react in anger, frustration, or fear. It's working through challenges as a team. It's encouraging each other's faith. It's showing gentleness, understanding, and compassion in times of stress. We wanted to do all this not just with each other but also intentionally in front of our future kids. We made a promise to always nurture our relationship, and I intended to keep it.

For our one-year dating anniversary, we spent the weekend at a family beach house. Rather than doing what normal couples do, like rubbing tanning lotion on each other's backs, swimming, and taking romantic walks on the beach, we found some burned pieces of charcoal lying on the beach and drew tribal designs on our faces. We stuck some bushy branches and seashells in our hair and then danced on the beach for the next hour.

Now that I am telling this story, it sounds a little odd, but it showed that I could let my guard down with her. If a relationship is going to be sustainable through marriage, it's important to be comfortable being fully yourself around each other. It helps if you actually enjoy hanging out, which may seem obvious. We didn't need distractions like television or our phones to fill our time together; we were fully focused on each other, and we could never get enough.

For our first Valentine's Day, I took the children's book *Harold and the Purple Crayon* and rewrote it to tell our story just three months after we shared those first "I love yous." I drew over the pictures with a black Sharpie and cut out tiny pieces of paper to tape over the original words. I detailed how we met and went on to tell of us getting married and having lots of babies and grandkids, all while walking with Jesus to accomplish great things in life.

### RACHEL

It was the most thoughtful, unique, and creative gift I've ever been given. We were both so confident and comfortable with each other that writing about getting married and having kids together, only months after meeting and after seeing each other in person maybe four times, was somehow romantic instead of completely presumptuous and creepy.

Dating long distance forced us to work a little harder and a little more creatively to make our love known when we weren't together in person. We went above and beyond for each other not because we had to but because we wanted to. This intentionality helped us lay a strong foundation as we learned early on that love is a choice that requires action.

One such effort occurred when I flew up to see Harold the evening before the Army-Navy baseball games on April 1, 2013. This was the first and only time I had any real doubt in our relationship. The doubt wasn't because of us but because of fear that his family didn't like me, specifically his sister, Liz.

She was really struggling with their parents' divorce and had started to feel like she was losing her brother too because he and I were in such a serious relationship. I knew how important family was to Harold, and I didn't want to cause a rift between them. It broke me. When you love someone, you want the best for them, so I doubted my place with Harold if his sister didn't like me.

Instead of ignoring the issue, Harold and I stayed up all night talking and crying our hearts out on the eve of one of the most important games of his life. That single night could have torn us apart, but instead, communication saved us. We recommitted to deepening our relationship and working through such doubts together. My relationship with his sister got better, by the way, and it's great now.

I learned through that turmoil that I needed to acknowledge my unreasonable expectation of perfection, for myself and others. In relationships, it's important to extend grace and let go of unrealistic expectations. I'll be the first to admit that at times I put too much pressure on people, including myself, to be perfect. The truth is, that's a pressure we aren't designed to bear. Relationships require understanding.

## HAROLD

We lost both games of the doubleheader the next day. In fact, I went 0–7 at the plate. But it was worth it because I didn't lose Rachel. We were tested, and it almost broke us. We intentionally took the time to communicate and align our priorities. We bent, but we didn't break. Holding Rachel after that loss, I didn't feel like I had really lost anything at all.

My relationship with Rachel was teaching me about effective communication. I had a lot to learn, especially about how I was communicating with God, which is the simplest yet hardest thing to do. Why is that? Short answer: If I struggle at actively communicating with Rachel, Soldiers on a military mission, or even getting my dog to sit for a treat, all of whom can talk (or bark) back, then how will I be good at communicating with Someone I can't see or hear?

Combine that with how the cultural norm for communication demands instantaneous responses. When I am texting someone about a problem, I can see when my message is delivered and read, and I can even see little bubbles when that person is responding. I think we often wish the same tracking system could be used with God. We want . . . we expect . . . no, we demand, actually, to see "read" beneath the 11:54 a.m. note, followed by an instant reply from God with direction on how to solve our problem. But God doesn't work this way, and since we can't see Him, it can feel like no one is listening on the other end. It's like a kid who is talking on an old telephone with a cord attached to it, but the cord has been cut and is dangling at his feet.

To be honest, a few years back, I seriously questioned whether God communicated with us at all. It wasn't that I didn't believe in Him; I just never heard Him speak to me. I would pray but hear no response. I would go to church but not feel Him working in my life. All too often, I felt like that kid with the dangling cord. I was skeptical then, but I can attest today that I am living proof God does respond. While it may not be in the typical way we receive responses from our friends, God speaks to us. We just need to listen in the right way to hear Him.

April 19, 2016

The "death zone" is the part of Everest above 26,247 feet. Everyone must enter the zone to reach the summit, roughly 3,000 feet higher. Basically, you are dying while you are up that high. Nothing is working as it should, and that's a tremendous strain on anyone's body, no matter how old or what kind of shape you're in. The lack of oxygen is simply killing you. No one can stay in the death zone for long—ideally, no more than one night.

Add an accident or moment of poor judgment, and it can easily mean the end, whether it involves you or someone else. Many have died trying to help their friends, teammates, or even complete strangers. There's an unwritten code that if you get into trouble in the death zone, you can't expect others to successfully help you, because it's extremely dangerous (and virtually impossible) to attempt a rescue at that altitude. It's likely you'll be left to die a lonely death.

Despite that unwritten code, everybody on our team has decided we will do everything in our power to help one another get down the mountain or attempt a rescue if needed. Our climbing team, called USX (US Expeditions and Explorations), is part of a bigger Western guide service called Summit Climb, and it includes sixteen people from all across the US and Europe. Our team includes Dr. Dave Ohlson, our team doctor and cinematographer from Anchorage, Alaska, and Staff Sergeant Chad Jukes (ret.) from Colorado, who is a combat-wounded amputee looking to be the first combat-wounded veteran to summit Everest.

He lost his leg to an IED in Iraq. Both men are renowned climbers. The rest of the team come primarily from across the Midwest.

Dave gives us a small bottle of adrenaline and a needle. We are to tape them to our left inside chest pocket so we all know where to find them on each climber. Our body heat keeps it from freezing. We have two doses to use only in extreme situations, such as if one of us snaps a leg and has to rappel down one of the several cliff faces near the summit. Each shot lasts ten minutes. Dave says it makes you feel like Superman and then you crash hard. We have steroids and other essential medications strapped to us as well. Climbers even take Viagra because it improves blood flow and promotes oxygenation, which makes it easier to breathe.

After seeing this intimidating mountain, I can't help but think about the real possibility of dying. Tommy and I talk about this, and while we mostly joke about it, at one point I become serious.

"Hey, man. If anything happens, make sure you take care of Rachel. If Rachel is pregnant, I want you to be the godfather."

I say this in a half-joking way, but we both know the gravity of my words. I've already talked to my sister and "jokingly" left her in charge of my funeral if I don't make it back. Before leaving, I increased my Army life insurance, maxing it out at $400,000.

Staring at Everest, I'm actually glad to have done all those things. I still plan to record an "in case I don't come home" message for Rachel up on the mountain—a message I hope and pray she'll never have to listen to.

# 4

A Million Times Yes

**RACHEL**

On February 1, 2014, I received a mass text message from my sorority:

Roses are red, violets are blue, someone is engaged, let's find out who.

Each time a girl in my sorority got engaged, she would tell only our president. The president would then host a "candlelight," where all the sisters would stand in a circle and pass around a burning candle. After it passed the circle three times, the newly engaged girl would blow it out when it came around to her, and that's how everyone would learn who it was.

After reading the text, I was selfishly upset. I was so ready for it to be my turn! Harold and I had been dating for almost a year and a half. Had he not been at West Point, we probably would have been married already. But West Point has a rule that you can't get married until after you graduate. Dating for a year and a half seems like a normal amount of time before getting engaged, but for us it felt like *forever*. I was expecting it to happen at any moment—at least at any moment that we had planned to see each other—but Harold was back at West Point coming down with a cold.

The next morning, I was still curled up under the covers when my roommate flicked on the lights and told me I had to get up because the candlelight was happening soon. I had zero desire to get ready, but since my friend Lauren had invited me to an event right after the ceremony, I had to put on a dress and look half decent. I couldn't find my shoes, so I was about to go downstairs barefoot when my roommate threw her shoes at me and said, "Just wear mine!"

When I walked downstairs, everyone was staring at me. They assumed it was my candlelight because everyone knew how crazy in love Harold and I were. This only made me more annoyed because to my knowledge, it was *not* my candlelight.

We all stood in a circle on the back patio and sang a song as we passed around the candle, waiting for someone to blow it out. When it passed me for the third time, I held it and couldn't help thinking the obvious. *See! It isn't me!*

But then BAM! Into the circle walked Harold. The moment I saw his face, my eyes were like a faucet with a continuous stream of tears. I knew this was our moment. He wrapped his arm around my waist and gave the sweetest speech; then he dropped to one knee while opening a box he had made out of a *Harold and the Purple Crayon* book. Inside was a gorgeous engagement ring.

I was blown away by the effort Harold had put into making that moment so special for us, and, boy, did I feel loved. It's one thing to say we love each other, but being intentional about showing that love is just as important. Actions make words meaningful.

## HAROLD

Unbeknownst to Rachel, I had called the president of her sorority and set up a candlelight before we were engaged. Then I told Rachel an elaborate lie about how I was feeling sick and was going to sleep the day away in my barracks room. I knew she would expect me to propose if we made plans to see each other, so I needed to keep her guessing. After taking a ferry, train, and two airplanes, I was halfway across the country, hiding at her sorority house without her even knowing!

I had learned my lesson from when we first met, and I recruited help from Rachel's friend Lauren to make sure Rachel got ready this time. Then, during the ceremony, as the candle was being passed around, I snuck up and stood behind her. As the candle slowly made its way to Rachel, I stepped in front of her, took the candle, blew it out, and dropped to one knee. A bunch of squeals and high-pitched "awwwws" ensued from around the circle. My mind was racing; I had so much I wanted to say. This is a little of what came out:

"Sweetie, I want to have a family with you. I want to have lots of kids with you, lots of little Harolds running around. Sweetie, I want to make love to you every night and wake up in the morning and make love to you again. Sweetie, I want to grow old with you. Sweetie, it will be tough, it won't always be easy, but I promise I'll make you the happiest woman in the world. Rachel, will you make me the happiest man on earth? Rachel Wynn, will you marry me?"

**RACHEL**

Yes, yes, *yes! A million times yes!*

**April 21, 2016**

Frenzied activity and a miniature city of brightly colored tents of all sizes cover a wide open rocky plain. I arrive at Everest Base Camp on a sunny day with clear skies and temperatures in the forties. Dozens of climbers surround me, some moving with purpose, others relaxing by their tents. Sherpas are everywhere, each busy carrying gear, food, bottles of oxygen and water, and other supplies. I scurry out of the way as Sherpas guide yaks with bells around their necks, toting climbing gear. I feel like a kid who is roaming the streets of some city he doesn't know. Straight ahead, beyond the city of tents, stands my nemesis. Everest stares me down.

At camp, we meet our Sherpa team. They have weathered faces and rough hands yet friendly smiles. The Sherpa people are an ethnic group native to the Himalayan mountains. They're known for their mountaineering expertise. They can handle altitude better than most people and know the routes well. Many climbers hire a Sherpa to ascend Everest with them, helping with gear, oxygen, and overall safety. They speak in broken English but are a joy to interact with. They, too, have families they are leaving behind.

I'm introduced to An Doja, my Sherpa, who has summited Everest five times and has a family back home. I shake his hand and tell him I'm looking forward to working with him. As he smiles, his kindness shines through his rough, callused skin. An Doja is an absolute animal at climbing with heavy gear. As we talk, we both have a serious look in our eyes. He knows that over the next thirty days I'm going to be putting my life and my future in his hands, just as he'll be putting his in mine.

I'm not afraid to admit I need his help if I want to be successful on Everest. Even though I've spent the past year rock climbing and training almost every day, An Doja has wisdom that I do not possess. He will show me the value of leaning on someone who has more experience. This isn't the time to let my pride get in the way of reaching out for help. I know my personal strengths (my physical fitness, health, and youth), and I know my weaknesses (my inexperience, nominal technical-climbing skills, and limited knowledge of routes). I need someone whose strengths bolster my weaknesses. I need An Doja. Just like I need Rachel to check my pride, keep me balanced, and demonstrate what selfless love looks like.

We each choose our tents and pick up our gear. I lug my three bags, weighing about sixty pounds each, to my site.

The altitude is about seventeen thousand feet, and already I am panting. I can't move nearly as fast as I'm used to. I have to stop and take breaks, sitting on my bags to catch my breath. For a brief moment, I can't help but think the obvious: If I'm out of breath now, what's it going to be like at the top?

# A Dangerous Dream

## HAROLD

I remember it like yesterday. I was lying in bed at West Point, daydreaming and looking over my bucket list. Close to the top was "Become an American Soldier."

When I was young, we would go on family vacations to Washington, DC, and visit the Tomb of the Unknown Soldier. Seeing those Soldiers in uniform and learning about the selfless service the unknown Soldier represented inspired me. So much so that in sixth grade, when given the prompt "Write About Your Hero," my answer was obvious: an American Soldier. Since I would be commissioned as an Army officer when I graduated, I was almost ready to check this off the list.

Also on my list: "Play baseball at West Point." I could check that one off! While I didn't write them down, the two most important ones were "Get married" and "Have a family." One of those items was soon to have a check mark too.

In bold at the very top of my list was "Climb Mount Everest." As my eyes focused on this line item, I didn't think about my zero climbing experience, nor that I was from the great state of Georgia, where our tallest mountain stands fewer than five thousand feet. But suddenly, I couldn't get climbing Everest out of my head, even though I had always hated the cold and was terrible at running hills during PT in the Army.

I knew it wasn't a mountain for the inexperienced. It is a deadly beast. Although I would need a lot of training, I wanted to put myself in that extreme environment, in the death zone, to see what I was truly made of. I wanted to try to beat the thing I'm weakest at, and that's why Everest was number one on my list. It was a mind-consuming idea that I just couldn't ignore.

I had an unshakable feeling God was speaking to me, and that burning desire only became stronger whenever I thought of Everest. I knew I had to go.

I first mentioned Everest to Rachel over the phone when we were discussing our planned trip to the Serengeti to visit the Maasai tribe. Rachel and I had been trying to make it happen for a month, but it didn't look like it was going to pan out. This is when I decided to tell her my new plan.

"I've decided I'm going to climb Mount Everest."

"What?" she let out with a chuckle. "Why am I not surprised?"

Her response wasn't quite what I'd expected. I was expecting some apprehension and pushback. We spoke about it for a few minutes, and to my surprise, she didn't seem phased at all.

**RACHEL**

When Harold told me about his dream to climb Everest, I thought it was interesting. Not interesting as in intriguing, but interesting because he had never climbed a mountain before and it seemed pretty miserable to me. It wasn't until Harold surprised me with a trip to Canada to celebrate our two-year dating anniversary that I finally began to understand the gravity of his decision.

On the last day of the trip, as we drove back from Canada to

West Point, we had a long and thorough discussion about Everest. It was in that moment that I realized his mind was made up and he was all in, so I had an endless amount of questions.

"So, how long will you be gone?"

"Around two months," he said.

"And how dangerous is it going to be?"

He gave me a confident smile. "Pretty dangerous."

"How are you going to pay for this?"

He explained his plans, saying who he'd reach out to and how he wanted to proceed. I was doing my best to try to gain an understanding of what was going on in that mind of his.

## HAROLD

On the trip home from Canada, I could tell by Rachel's questions that this Everest thing was sinking in. I told her I'd already done some research; that is, I had googled "climbing Everest." I wondered, *How much does it cost? Have any Soldiers done it? When is the best time to climb?* Those questions caused me to think, *Can I put together an Army team? How incredible would that be? Is it even possible for an Army Soldier to do it?*

The next day I started emailing anybody and everybody who might have an interest in helping me make this dream a reality. I didn't know which direction to head, so I just sent out a shotgun blast in every direction to see what got traction.

One of the biggest obstacles people encounter once they decide to go after their dreams is not knowing how to start. Are you ready for the answer? Make a move, any move at all. It doesn't matter how big or small. Just do it. Take ten minutes and start doing something to make your dream happen; chances are you won't stop after just ten minutes. The sheer fact of starting makes it easier to continue because you're no longer staring at a blank slate.

Now, say you take your first step, but you don't go anywhere. Then what? Well, now it's easier to take the second step because at least you know where not to step. Keep going until something works. It's all about momentum. Once you get the ball moving, it's easier to steer it where you want it to go. With Everest, I knew only the end state I was aiming for; all the stuff in between I figured out by trial and error.

## RACHEL

Not only were we enduring a long-distance relationship and planning a wedding, but Harold was also adding Everest into the mix. While we were apart, we certainly saw our share of obstacles and challenges! Long distance is hard. It's a weird balance of having to be strong and independent enough to endure the distance yet vulnerable enough to move deeper in the relationship.

One thing that helped us get through the distance was doing our best to always make plans for the next time we would see each other. Since we got to see each other once a month at most, it was helpful to have something to look forward to. Dating long distance isn't sustainable if you don't have an end goal in mind; it will only drive you crazy. This really helped us keep up the morale of our relationship instead of dwelling on the fact that we weren't together. It's similar to the different seasons of a person's life. They're called seasons because there is supposed to be a beginning and an end. If you find yourself in a season that never ends, it's probably time to make a change. You can run for only so long before needing to slow down, rest, and recharge.

We learned that sharing our schedules with each other was one of the most important ways to prevent frustration and hurt feelings. When we failed to share our schedules, it always resulted in unmet expectations. For example, we normally talked on the phone in the evening, so if I called Harold and he didn't pick up or text me that night, I would feel hurt and confused. But if he let me know ahead of time that he would be at a study group and wouldn't be able to talk, I would be completely fine.

Another tactic that kept us united while we were apart was to work on projects together. While Harold's interest in climbing Everest skyrocketed, I helped him make lists, did research, and supported him in every way I could.

Being in a long-distance relationship is no walk in the park. Some days it felt a little like climbing Everest! But it also made the moments we were together so much sweeter and allowed our love to grow exponentially.

## HAROLD

Rachel was supportive in so many ways during this time, including helping me do research about climbing Everest. And there was a lot to know. One day I came across an article about an Army captain named CPT Matt Hickey who had notable climbing experience and had recently led an all-Army team to the summit of Denali with the Northern Warfare Training Center in Alaska.

*This guy is a stud*, I thought.

On impulse, I sent him an email, and to my surprise, he said he was available for a call. During our forty-five-minute conversation, he asked me a lot of questions: "What does your climbing experience look like? How high have you been?"

"I have none," I responded. "Well, actually, when I was a kid, I walked to the top of Brasstown Bald in Georgia. That's like five thousand feet."

There was an awkward silence. Matt suggested I prepare myself by climbing some peaks in the coming year. While he explained I had a lot of work to do, he did think it was possible. This was eye opening because I found that if you are passionate about something, people will often follow you or help you out, sometimes just out of curiosity.

Not everyone would be so encouraging or helpful, though. I received one email from an instructor of mine at West Point that made it clear there was no possible way I could climb Everest:

It's too dangerous, too expensive, and you'll never get it approved. I ap-
plaud [your] efforts but it won't happen. . . . I don't think you should focus
on this right now as a cadet.

That was harsh. I printed out the email and pasted it on my
wall in my barracks room for inspiration. By that time, I had already put in so much work that instead of the negative comments
causing self-doubt, they just stoked the fire within me, causing it
to burn hotter.

At this point, the only person who really encouraged me other
than Matt was Rachel, which was kind of backward since she had
the most to lose. I was jeopardizing our relationship and our future
by working toward this goal. I was a twenty-two-year-old cadet. I
had no real reason to think I could do it. But I thought I could. And
Rachel thought I could too.

I began reading everything about Everest I could get my hands
on, both online and in books. One small guidebook I picked up
started with this: "Everest is a deadly mountain. Anyone who thinks
otherwise has never been there or will never return. Although you
will learn a lot on Everest, think of the climb as a severe and possible
fatal final test, not a training ground." I guess the author wanted
to make sure people knew what they were getting into. The next
paragraph wasn't much more encouraging, listing in a concise and
emotionless tone a few of the dangers:

- A full Everest expedition takes up to two months, and most
  of that time you will feel unwell, while surrounded only by
  rocks and ice.
- You cross huge crevasses on treacherous ladders and go from
  boiling hot to incredibly cold temperatures within hours.
- There is a high risk of frostbite, and you can't count on
  evacuation.
- Your life is threatened most of the time; if you reach high

altitude, you will see and walk past the dead bodies of other climbers.*

Another piece of information that caught my attention was that the top of Mount Everest is in the jet stream, a series of atmospheric highways five to nine miles above sea level. With Everest sitting 29,029 feet high,** the summit is often lashed by these ferocious winds. There is a window of time in the late spring, mostly in May, when the weather is more predictable, making it the safest time to climb to the summit. If you go too early, you can freeze or get blown off the mountain in a matter of minutes. Timing is everything.

I started to stress, and when I stress, I feel that everything has to happen *right now*. However, faith is the reassurance in waiting for God's timing. My favorite Bible verse, Proverbs 16:9, says, "A man's heart plans his way, but the LORD directs his steps."

I would come to learn the truth of that verse in my relationship with Rachel—and with the weather on Everest. Sometimes the hard way. It just took a little time to figure it out.

---

* Harry Kikstra, *Everest: Summit of the World* (Massachusetts: Interlink Pub Group, 2009), 7.
** This is a widely recognized height, but many sources suggest the height is 29,035 feet. See Bhadra Sharma and Kai Schultz, "How Tall Is Mount Everest? For Nepal, It's a Touchy Question," *New York Times*, February 3, 2018, www.nytimes.com/2018/02/03/world/asia/mount-everest-how-tall-nepal.html.

The moment I hear Rachel's voice, I realize just how much I miss her. I haven't felt this tug during the day because of all the activity in camp. But as I FaceTime her for the first time, lying in my sleep sack at Base Camp, I can feel her love radiating across the miles.

Her laugh is the best, I think as we talk.

Rachel's laugh starts with a cute little giggle as her smile lines grow, and her grin spreads from ear to ear before she bursts into uncontrollable laughter. Even in the Chinese 2G, low-res, granulated picture, her smile is infectious. I can't help but grin back at her. Sometimes the image freezes or part of her teeth glitch and move to the middle of her forehead, but I don't care. I can't help taking screenshots left, right, and center. She is so gorgeous.

I was nervous earlier in the day when our team pulled out our advanced military-grade communication equipment and we couldn't get a signal immediately. It turns out, however, since I have T-Mobile, I get service at Base Camp. Odd, considering I feel like T-Mobile is more like T-Maybe in the States!

We're both so excited to talk to each other that I don't care it's costing me twenty cents a minute. It reminds me of our first phone conversation, one that went late into the night because neither of us wanted to hang up since we both had so much to say. Now we speak as fast as we can, interrupting each other, stopping midsentence to say, "I love you." The whole time, we talk in our cutesy voices, the ones that we use only around each other and that probably wouldn't make sense to anybody else. We actually have a name for our special language. We call it our WOW language because we start all our words with a w so "our" language sounds like "wow" language. Of course, I would be embarrassed if my fellow Soldiers or mountaineers heard me now, but it's a natural way we express our love. My heart longs to be with her again. I'd give anything to have her here in my tent with a flashlight brightening our faces while we giggle at the foot of the world's tallest mountain.

# Short End of the Stick

**RACHEL**

Six months after our engagement, Harold was neck deep in figuring out a plan to make his Everest dream a reality. It was that "can't eat, can't sleep, work through the night, figure out how to bring it up in every conversation" kind of love and determination. I found it inspiring, but it also meant our very limited time talking was now basically cut in half. I shared my fiancé with West Point, baseball, and now Everest.

I was learning that love has to be the main response when it comes to accomplishing big goals. Love is the strongest driving force, which is required when you take on an audacious dream. Without love of what you're pursuing, it's too easy to give up when you encounter obstacles. If you don't love it, is it really worth pursuing in the first place?

Many people have dreams, but how many actually make their dreams a reality? Especially the big, over-the-top, scary dreams that seem impossible? Most let fear stop them before they even get started by listening to lies like, *It's way too hard; it'll cost more money than I have; I'd probably fail anyway; I don't have what it takes.* So they just let their dreams die before even giving them a chance. I want to shake those people and say, "Stop selling yourselves short and push past those fears and lies! You are capable! You were made for greatness, but you have to step into it. You can't just dream about accomplishing goals or they will never happen. Work for them!"

Climbing Everest may have been slightly insane, but I truly admired Harold's determination. That level of drive isn't something seen every day. It opened my eyes to realize that often people's biggest obstacle is themselves.

Since Everest was Harold's dream, it needed to be my dream too. I wasn't going to just sit on the sidelines cheering him on. I needed to show up for him and make sure he knew I was in the game with him. Not only would Harold have a stronger chance of making his Everest dream happen if I was on his team, but we would also come out stronger as a couple if we faced this challenge together.

But let's be clear: my independent and driven self wouldn't have done this for just anyone; it was because he was the right one, my soon-to-be husband.

## HAROLD

My love for Rachel grew exponentially during this time. I didn't understand why she was being so supportive because, honestly, I don't think I would have been supportive if it were the other way around.

Have you gotten the short end of the stick before? I hate to admit it, but that's exactly what I was giving Rachel during my whole pursuit of Everest. People asked me how I got to be on the team to climb Everest, and I told them I created the team. Then they usually followed up with "How did you have time, especially at West Point with a full academic load while playing baseball?" The answer was that it required a tremendous amount of sacrifice by those closest to me, namely Rachel.

What was most impressive wasn't the support she gave me but

how she poured her heart into my dream. That is the sign of a true teammate, best friend, and lover. She would stay up later than I would sketching logo ideas, editing video content, and helping me go over gear checklists. Being committed to your spouse is expected in a marriage, but Rachel's commitment to my dreams and aspirations showed me just how much she cared about "us."

There's a good chance I would have lost my way if it hadn't been for Rachel. She kept me anchored in reality. She also let me know when I was getting full of myself and brought me back to earth.

We both have big dreams and strive to achieve them, but if all else fails and we lose everything, we will still be happy because we have each other. We could literally live with next to nothing, move to the wilderness, paint our faces with charcoal, and be happy sitting around a campfire eating squirrels together.

There I was, trying my best to find balance by being fully present in the moment, but I was failing. My priorities needed to be God, Rachel, West Point, my baseball team, and then the Everest expedition. In reality, it was the opposite: Everest, baseball, West Point, Rachel, and God.

I still struggle with this today. When I have an idea I think is worth pursuing, I get this mentality of *I'm sorry, Rachel, I just don't have time for you right now. I have a plan to save the world,* which is basically telling her that what I am doing is more important than she is. It certainly wasn't the mind-set I should've had toward my future wife.

A comment Dan Pallotta made during a TED Talk really hit home. He said,

> Too often our dreams become these compartmentalized fixations on some future that destroy our ability to be present for our lives right now . . . and alienate us from [other] human beings sitting next to us at this very moment.*

* Dan Pallotta, "The Dream We Haven't Dared to Dream," February 2016, TED

I was experiencing that firsthand, and Rachel was on the receiving end of it.

I spent most of my life thinking about and praying about what my future wife would look like and what it would be like when I had a family. Now that I'd found Rachel, I'm embarrassed to say how easily I took her for granted. People are always consumed with what they don't have instead of what they do have.

I already had the one thing in life I wanted most, but naturally, I started wanting and pursuing other things. I started to neglect what was most valuable to me. Now I know it is so very important to frequently take a step back to reflect and see the bigger picture. To ask what is really most important in life. What do I really care about? What would I want to hold on to if all else faded? At the time, I never asked myself those questions because they probably would have shifted how I prioritized my life and how I appreciated Rachel.

## RACHEL

It was my goal to see Harold's goal come to life. I made sacrifices out of love for him. Knowingly giving up quality time with him was the hardest. I figured out he would be away for two months during the actual climb and before then on several occasions to train or raise money. Not to mention all the weeknights and weekends that were devoted to school and work. He would use all his leave time, and then some, for the expedition and would end up with negative forty-five days of leave. This meant we wouldn't have vacation time in the foreseeable future.

Some days the thought of Everest killed me, and some days I was impressed by my strength. If I had taken the approach that this was *his* goal and I wanted nothing to do with it, I believe it probably would have torn us apart. There really would have been no way for

Talk, 11:49, www.ted.com/talks/dan_pallotta_the_dream_we_haven_t_dared_to_dream/transcript?language=en.

us to have a healthy relationship while he pursued Everest had I made the decision not to support him.

Harold made sacrifices for me too. He had always wanted to do Special Forces, which meant he would be deployed behind enemy lines. It's not the most family-friendly job and would have required him to be gone a lot. This made me feel super uneasy. I never told Harold he couldn't do Special Forces, but as a sacrifice for me, he chose not to. I know if we hadn't gotten together, that's the path he would have chosen. Making sacrifices is an act of love. It shows your partner that you choose to be together even if it requires an unfavorable situation for you.

Harold and I always remind each other that we have a lifetime to work toward our dreams and we don't have to make them happen all at once. We are working to reach our goals together. In relationships, it's important to remember the reason behind what you're both working toward. What is it that you both want most out of life? What kind of life are you trying to build together? For Harold and me, our ultimate cause is to live a fulfilling life full of love while using our gifts to bring glory to God. We live by a little saying I came up with: "Love God, love people, make a difference, and be thankful." Our hope is to live a life that exemplifies those actions and inspires other people to do the same.

As his pursuit of Everest picked up speed, I began to worry that Harold was leaving God out of it. I knew he could accomplish great feats, but I was nervous he was getting so wrapped up in his own plans that he wasn't intentionally pursuing God through them.

## HAROLD

I'm not good at stopping and asking God what I should do. I just go and don't pause. I don't know for sure that God is actually speaking to me every time I get a strong desire. I'm more like 52 percent sure. I must discern each call, being careful to not listen to my ego or selfish desires but rather to learn to hear God's voice the loudest.

I've learned over time and by making many wrong decisions with good intentions that my heart must first be focused on Him to see the signs He's giving me.

Even if I'm not necessarily pursuing God, He is always pursuing me. Sometimes He works through other people to speak truth into our lives, which is exactly what happened with one of my mentors. I met Command Sergeant Major Todd Burnett in basic training when he came up to me one morning and made me do push-ups because my socks weren't pulled up straight enough.

"Why aren't those socks motivated, cadet? They're sagging like your back when you do push-ups." As soon as I dropped to the ground, he dropped down next to me and said, "Let's see how many you can do!"

I proceeded to do more push-ups than I had in my entire life, and I started to get tired.

"Come on! Is that all you can do?" he said as he continued to rep out push-ups and smack-talk me the whole time.

When I got up, he put his arm around me and said, "Nice work, Soldier." CSM Burnett has a scar across his face and looks like he fought the entire Iraq War by himself. He's in incredible shape for his age. I watched as he walked over to another new cadet. "That shirt is three sizes too big; let's help you fill it out," he said as he began doing push-ups again. I smiled in disbelief. *Who is this man?*

A cadre trainer later told me that he knew someone who had served with CSM Burnett and that he was once shot in the helmet twice in one day.

He was a big baseball fan and came to nearly every practice. Over the next three years, we built a strong bond; he became a mentor to me in leadership, my spiritual life, and my family. So, when he asked me a question about Everest, I listened.

"Harold, you talk about what you are wanting to do by climbing Mount Everest, but why are you doing it? Is there a nexus to all this?"

I didn't have an answer other than that climbing Everest was something I'd always wanted to do, I felt God calling me to it, and it would be historic for the Army.

"What if you climb for a cause?" he said. "You could climb for awareness about post-traumatic stress disorder."

I was a young Soldier and had no idea what PTSD really looked like or how deeply it affected our military ranks. If I'm being completely transparent, I ashamedly thought climbing for a cause could possibly bring in more money and lend credibility to what we were doing. It wasn't until months later when I heard more of CSM Burnett's personal story and stories of other American heroes like him that I learned the tragic impact PTSD has on our service members. Death by suicide was claiming the lives of one active-duty Soldier a day and twenty-two veterans a day. My heart was broken.

When CSM Burnett told me about his struggles with PTSD, the climb took on new meaning. He had been through a lot of personal tragedies, including the deaths of his brothers. One had recently been killed in a motorcycle accident; the other committed suicide just a month later. I've dealt with only one family death, my grandfather's, and it crushed me. I can't even imagine his heartache of losing two brothers, in addition to the numerous brothers and sisters he'd lost in combat.

CSM Burnett's struggle with PTSD intensified to the point of wanting to take his own life. I sat and listened to my hero, an incomparable warrior and someone many of us looked up to, say he'd wanted to kill himself due to PTSD. I was speechless. The reason behind climbing Everest became very real to me in that instant. My drive to make the expedition happen shifted from self-centered motives to something much bigger.

I was no longer climbing for myself; now I was climbing for my brothers and sisters who were struggling. I made it my mission to create awareness of PTSD so that resources and encouragement would be provided to veterans in the midst of climbing their own mountains of adversity. All the sacrifices Rachel and I were making would be worth it if we could save just one life.

God was communicating with me more clearly than ever, and it was through a man I looked up to. Thankfully, I was listening in the right way to hear it.

After several days of acclimatization, I'm accustomed
to more than just the thin air. I'm used to the same Base
Camp breakfast: donkey meat medallions, eggs, and po-
tatoes cooked in yak grease, served with toast and butter
made from yak milk. Tomorrow we'll be heading up to
Interim Camp and then on to Everest's Advanced Camp.

Acclimatization on Everest is extremely important. This
process allows the body to start adjusting to the high altitude while gaining the strength needed to climb. We begin
the process immediately, climbing a section, coming back
to rest, and then repeating the process. Each time our goal
is to climb a little higher.

Many climbers who die on Everest get a common illness, like a head cold or stomach bug, but decide to climb
anyway, even though the illness rapidly accelerates the
body's deterioration with every step in elevation. Before
leaving, I told myself that if I were confronted with a situation that would considerably increase my risk, I would turn
around and stop climbing. This is not a hard decision when
I have a beautiful new bride back home, but for others, it's
not always an obvious decision.

Staring up at the mountain, it is easy for me to focus
solely on completing the goal: make it to the top and back
down. Amid this intense focus, there are a few lighthearted
moments.

This morning, Tommy leaves our yak-filled breakfast to
go to the bathroom at the toilet pit. The toilet pit is exactly

what it sounds like: a six-foot hole with a tent draped over it for privacy. I'm finishing breakfast when Tommy starts yelling. I run over to the toilet tent to see what's happening.

"Tom, you all right?"

"My water bottle fell in a pile of poop!"

"Did you get it?"

"No, I left it there!"

Dave and Chad, two of the guys on our USX team, hear what's going on and come over. One of them says, "You need to get it out. It's not right to leave it there."

Tommy knows they're right, so he heads back in to retrieve his water bottle. Dave and Chad go with him for moral support.

Somehow Tommy gets it out using a string and a stick. When we see the bottom of the water bottle covered in poop with toilet paper stuck on it, all of us start rolling with laughter. The Sherpas do too. They feel sorry for Tommy and help him clean it off using buckets of hand sanitizer. Later, when the team goes to the mess tent for dinner, Tommy unthinkingly sets his water bottle on the table. We eye it suspiciously. I guess it's clean, but it still doesn't seem right to have it so close to our food!

After dinner, I talk to Rachel. We have a good laugh about the poo story. From this point forward, the laughs will be few and far between. We both know it will probably be a week before we can talk again. The team is leaving to climb up to the more dangerous higher camps at first light. But for the moment, I focus solely on Rachel and her sweet laugh as my bride's love radiates through me, warming me on this cold, dark night on the side of the mountain.

# When Nothing Is Certain, Everything Is Possible

**RACHEL**

As we worked toward making this whole Everest adventure come to life, it ignited this spark to look back over my own childhood dreams. Of course, my biggest desires were to find love and to one day have a family, which were now starting to happen, but I had other dreams too. If we could work together to see Harold's Everest dream come to life, what was to say the same couldn't happen for my dreams? So, I started to reminisce about what paths and decisions had led me to where I was at that point in my life.

I had this entrepreneurial fire in me because I really liked the idea of being my own boss and having the freedom to create my own path. I had always really enjoyed baking, so the thought of owning my own bakery someday was a fun idea. During my junior year of high school, I started my own little culinary business and named it Bite-Sized Delights. One of my mom's best friends also had this amazing hydroponic farm, where I would occasionally help plant the fruit and work at the U-picks.

I bought strawberries directly from her that I used to make chocolate-covered strawberries and chocolate bowls full of fresh strawberries. My specialty, though, were Oreo cheesecake balls. I sold my creations to kids at school and family friends, and I even catered an event or two. I loved the freedom and excitement of being an entrepreneur even more than the money. The whole process felt empowering.

I feel our culture gets it backward and conveys the idea that money leads to happiness, but in reality, many people are unhappy because they spend so much time in jobs they hate simply because they earn a certain level of income. Money is a wonderful tool that can enable people, but living an unfulfilling life for the sake of money will leave them unsatisfied and complacent. I believe we were all made for more.

At that point, my path to the future didn't seem very clear. In fact, it was one cloudy mess with almost no visibility, and I had no clue what my professional goals should be. I wished I had a clear calling to become a lawyer or doctor or something, but all I really knew was that I wanted to work for myself, which would allow me to keep my family life a priority. I also knew I wanted to help people and make a positive difference in the world. I felt pressure from my family to continue down the business route in college. Sure, I wanted to own my own business someday, but was I passionate about business calculus and accounting? Not in the slightest. Taking all those classes meant I'd end up working in someone else's business and climb the corporate ladder. Not my idea of fun.

For the first time in my life, I experienced true anxiety. I'd cry on my way to my business classes or stay up all night studying something I hated and then cry at my campus church after I failed a test. Chasing after something I had no passion for left me feeling empty and anxious.

Failing wasn't something I did. I had always been an A student with a résumé piled high with academic honors, club involvements, and extracurricular activities. So, when I began to really struggle with my studies, I felt embarrassed and defeated. I was so embarrassed I didn't tell anyone how badly I was really doing. I began to feel a deep sense of shame, like somehow my school success was tied to my self-worth. I felt stuck. The fear of judgment and criticism was holding me back from fixing my situation.

I was incredibly unhappy trying to live up to other people's ideas of success. It took redefining what success means to me to be able to climb out of my hole of shame. I love the way Maya Angelou said it: "Success is liking yourself, liking what you do, and liking how you do it."*

I had to acknowledge that my self-worth was not, in fact, tied to my career path, my potential income, my achievements, or my level of success according to the world's standards. My internal joy would never be dependent on external measures. This is the reason I am so passionate about people never settling in any aspects of their lives. We often settle by pursuing what the world wants from us when it's not truly what we want for ourselves. If we all stopped living according to other people's timelines and expectations, we'd feel freer to take the reins of our own stories.

I reached out to my pastor and after some long talks realized I needed to switch my major to something else to preserve my own sanity. I thought about pursuing ministry and going to seminary after I graduated, but God kept showing me that my ministry was going to be outside the walls of a church. I switched to an interdisciplinary social sciences major and also ended up with minors in child development and religion simply because I enjoyed the classes so much.

What I couldn't see at the time was that what I perceived as a failure was just a turn in direction, which led to a happier me.

* Maya Angelou, quoted in Aberdin Louis, *Famous Success Quotes* (Brooklyn, NY: Let's Go Big Family, 2015), 75.

Failure isn't an end state. I chose to keep going and keep growing. I changed my major and still graduated on time with honors, while being significantly happier and free of anxiety.

## HAROLD

I remember on one of our video chats when we'd been dating for only a few months, Rachel told me she got a C in her math class. I made what I thought was a playful joke about it, and it led to a big argument. I immediately knew this was an area Rachel took seriously and had been struggling with for some time.

Rachel derives great joy and zeal for life from helping others and making a difference. When she told me she changed her major, it made sense. Business wasn't her passion. Rachel has such a pure heart, and it is the driving force behind how she pursues her life. She couldn't care less about the size of our home or the type of clothes she wears. I mean, she met me for the first time in that camo T-shirt, of all things. Not to call her out, but as we sit writing this book, I'm noticing that she has been wearing the same pair of baggy sweatpants for the past three days! But I love that about her.

Rachel has shown me that life is about serving rather than getting, doing rather than having, and being rather than wanting. She keeps me grounded in this way, building our marriage on a strong foundation of what is important. I may be the man and protector of the house, but she is our family's foundation. I learned I needed that foundation during my Firstie (senior) year at West Point after she had graduated.

During my final season of baseball, I ended up with a rear labral tear in my shoulder after diving for a ball. My injury was pretty devastating on all fronts. Obviously, it affected baseball (not just my playing but the whole team), and it also potentially affected Everest. How could I climb with a torn shoulder?

I decided to wait it out and play through the pain until the end of the season and then have surgery. It was an unfortunate situation, but it actually worked out in my favor. You see, I had been having a hard time figuring out how the Everest climb would work into my military timeline and obligations, but strangely enough, the surgery meant I would be classified as a MedHold during my recovery time, which then lined up my schedule and Everest perfectly. What a God thing hurting my shoulder turned out to be! As Rachel stated, a lot of times our failures end up leading us in better directions.

There were still a lot of pieces that had to fall into place, but more and more it seemed possible. We were about a year out at this point, and I estimated my chances of going at a generous 40 percent. We still needed to raise over $100,000. We were already starting to gain traction raising awareness about PTSD with an *Army Times* article about our efforts and cause. Momentum had started slowly but was now beginning to build.

Originally, I tried to get the US Army to officially approve the expedition but quickly learned that would not be possible. I then tried to get some other veteran organizations to help with funding, but they politely declined, saying it was too expensive and they didn't have full trust in a cadet's ability to make it happen.

That's when we decided to start our own nonprofit called US Expeditions and Exploration, or USX. We ended up raising more than six figures to fund the expedition, despite having zero business experience. How, you ask? Hustle. We rolled up our sleeves and got creative. It also gave us the ability to really focus our efforts on mental-health issues among Soldiers.

In hindsight, my time was occupied by so many things. I wish I would have been more of a spiritual leader for us, and I know Rachel wished it too. I struggled with having wrongfully overcommitted myself, and rather than growing in my faith, instead I only maintained it. I became so deliberate in planning for this climb and the safety of our team that I was negligent in planning for the safety of our marriage. Over the course of this year, I noticed Rachel started to seem unhappy.

## RACHEL

The first half of Harold's senior year brought back some of those same feelings of inadequacy I'd experienced before I even met him. I didn't want to take my frustration out on Harold, but I knew that if I was single, I could be anywhere, maybe at a new job somewhere else in the United States or even off on a cool adventure somewhere abroad. I could pursue anything I wanted.

But, at my core, building a life with Harold was the most important thing to me, even if it meant my life would take a very different turn. Still, I sometimes questioned if I was selling myself short by sacrificing my potential for work success with this upcoming Army-wife lifestyle. What was I getting myself into? Sure, I'd be happy in my marriage, but would struggles of inferiority follow me around and cause problems between us?

I knew I had to communicate to Harold what I was feeling because I had learned before that staying silent only did a disservice to myself and ultimately our relationship. He set me straight by reminding me that he would support anything I wanted to do and empowered me not to put limitations on myself.

In the midst of all this, I witnessed one of those childhood dreams of mine suddenly become a reality.

## HAROLD

The time apart was hard on us. We both felt a very intense longing to be with each other, but my senior year schedule made it tough. Rachel was always recording little videos on her phone about where she was and what she was up to and then sending them to me, which made me feel close to her. I loved hearing her voice.

I knew Rachel felt comfortable on camera and had been part of a video production team in middle and high school, so I thought of something she might enjoy doing.

"Why don't you start a YouTube channel?"

## April 27, 2016

As we climb higher up the mountain, more dangers present themselves. The sun, for example, can reflect off the surrounding glacial ice and cause blisters to form on the inside of your mouth as you pant for air. Dehydration is also a threat. As we climb, I see deep, dark crevasses snaking through the glaciers. People who fall into these crevasses are often there forever. Their bodies become preserved as frozen sculptures and are sometimes slowly crushed by the shifting of the glaciers over time.

The team and I make it to Advanced Base Camp, which is over twenty thousand feet in elevation, and we rest here briefly before traveling up the North Col, the one-thousand-foot vertical, sheer-ice wall. This will be the first time we get to strap on our crampons (sharp traction devices that look like spikes coming out of your shoes, which are used to gain stability on ice and glaciers), and we're all super excited!

After retrieving my gear from the yaks, I set up my lantern and picture of Rachel in my tent. I open the front zipper and take in the clear view of the summit of Everest . . . and the intense route we will be taking to get there. We have Camp One directly in front of us on top of the North Col. We can see climbers slowly moving up it, looking like a small line of ants.

Camp Two stands at the top of a long and gradual snow-banked slope. No technical climbing skills are needed for this part of the climb. It's essentially just a suck fest of a hike. Camp Three is where things get interesting.

It is perched at roughly twenty-seven thousand feet on the ridge face of the mountain. This is the intense, black, mean-looking part of the mountain that struck me when I first saw Everest. Camp Three stands right in the middle of the black. Moving from Camp Three to the summit is the most difficult part of the climb. The route is complicated to navigate, requiring traversing narrow ledges and dealing with the high wind and weather. The extreme altitude and thin air add complexity and danger to the already treacherous conditions.

I sit at the opening of my tent, looking up at nearly two miles of vertical height. An afternoon storm starts to swell in the distance. The summit of Everest quickly fades behind dark, ominous clouds. All of Everest and her fury stand in front of me.

# The West Point Girlfriend

**RACHEL**

When Harold mentioned YouTube, my ears perked up. I was substitute teaching occasionally, nannying, and working for a nonprofit, but I wanted more for myself. I'm so thankful Harold helped me find a way to reach my own dreams.

One dream that had stayed with me since the age six was having a television show. This dream is what led me to join the video production team in middle and high school. I used to pretend I had my own talk show called *The Rachel Show*, and later when I had a laptop and cell phone, I would record all kinds of embarrassing videos of me talking to an imaginary audience.

It all started when my brother and I were little and we went to visit our older sister, Julie, who was living on her own. She had this amazing black-and-white video camera with a long cord that attached to the television so we could watch ourselves while we were recording. That was the moment my six-year-old heart fell in love with videography.

My brother, Will, and I would stand in front of the television and dance, although I'd usually take over the show, going crazy while jumping up and down, shaking my curly hair, and spinning around. Will was slightly shyer and focused on drawing comics, so naturally, as the younger sibling, I would pester him, asking a million questions as I pretended to interview him on camera. "Go away, Rachel. I'm trying to draw," he'd say. But that was okay with me because my sis had the holy grail toy, an Easy-Bake Oven! In five seconds, I went from interviewing my brother about comics to having my own cooking show!

"This is a double chocolate chip doughnut cookie, and we're about to do the best part—SPRINKLESSSSS," I'd say as I did a silly dance. My catchphrase for the evening was to say in my high-pitched voice, "We're having so much fun!" Julie was a good sport and played along too, even ad-libbing commercials for the camera when I asked.

It's funny how our early years can be a reflection of who we become. I didn't know it at the time, but my childhood dream of having my own television show would, in a way, become a reality as I started sharing my life through online videos. This quickly became a new passion that would turn into my dream job.

The night Harold suggested I start a YouTube channel, I came up with a rough outline in my journal, pulled together a few props, and used the camera on my computer to make a video. I called it "Signs You're Dating a West Point Cadet."

"You have plenty of camo," I said, waving my camo-wearing teddy bear at the camera.

"Your boyfriend decides to serve you a super delicious MRE for breakfast." I rolled my eyes.

"Everyone stares at you when you walk onto campus in civilian clothes and with your hair down."

"You pick up random military terms, like *Roger* . . . *Copy* . . . *Over.*"

"Your boyfriend gets haircuts more often than you."

After a couple of takes and a quick edit, I showed it to Harold and my mom. I uploaded it to YouTube and posted a link on the West Point girlfriend support group on Facebook. I wasn't normally someone who was active in online groups—in fact, it may have been the first time I posted—but I thought someone might relate to my very cheesy video.

Within a couple of hours, a few hundred people had watched the video. When I woke up the next day, it had over seven thousand views. The girlfriends loved it! Unfortunately, some of the West Point cadets didn't, and they slammed me.

While a lot of people liked the video and felt it gave us girls a voice, there was also a ton of backlash. Some of my family members were even worried I was going to hurt Harold's career because of the negativity that initially surrounded it. I also received a couple of death threats in the comments. The internet can be a cruel place. One thing was for sure: whether people liked the video or not, almost every person at West Point now knew who I was.

I quickly became known as the West Point Girlfriend, rather than Rachel. It had a negative connotation, which made me feel weird and uncomfortable. The cadets would announce my arrival on campus whenever I visited. "West Point Girlfriend spotted in the parking lot" they'd post on an app called Yik Yak. Luckily, Harold is the greatest and seemed completely unfazed. He was supportive through all of it, reassuring me that he wasn't embarrassed but was actually really proud of me.

## HAROLD

I wanted to support Rachel in doing something she loved, but neither of us had any idea how this one video would blow up at West Point. I was sitting at my desk in the barracks doing some schoolwork that night when she sent me the video. "Oh, cool! I'm proud of you. That's great," I told her, and I went back to studying, not thinking any more of it.

That same evening, after thousands of people had already watched it and posted comments, a friend texted me and said, "Hey, man, are you doing all right?" I was like, "Yeah, man, thanks for asking," but I had no idea why he had randomly asked. Unbeknownst to me, the video was spreading like wildfire among the Corps of Cadets, who clustered on a few different social media apps and reacted to anything that caught their collective attention, especially related to school, girls, or school and girls. Later that night, two cadets knocked on my door that was already propped open.

"Are you Harold Earls?"

"Uhh, yeahhh."

They burst out laughing and stormed down the hall. I looked over at my roommate, completely bewildered, and then texted my friend back and asked, "What's going on?"

The next morning as I was walking through historic Thayer Hall to get to class, I heard a familiar voice echoing down the hallway. It was Rachel's voice coming through the sound system inside a classroom. The instructor was showing Rachel's video on the classroom projector! I was in shock and kept walking down the hallway, but then I saw it again and again in each classroom I passed. When I walked into my classroom to take my seat, my instructor was playing it too. The video was everywhere.

The backlash to the video didn't bother me. When the world disapproves of what you're doing, you may be doing something bold and extraordinary and people just don't realize it yet. I told Rachel to focus on the impact, not the approval.

Even when the world seems against us, Rachel and I have always had each other's back. I love that about us. I know it may be a tough fight, but my cornerman will always be there, showing up every day, saying, "I want you to know that I love you, I care about your future, and I've got your back through it all." Everyone, no matter how resilient, needs someone who will provide encouragement and warm reassurance along the way.

This is where true love lies, at the crossroads of continually supporting each other in the uncertainty and challenges of life and creating a path together filled with excitement, failure, and adventure. This is what I saw in Rachel's YouTube video. It was so much more than just a silly video. That's why I didn't pay much attention to the haters.

## RACHEL

Rather than letting the negativity discourage me, the fact that anyone was listening to what I had to say empowered me. I felt like I was finding my voice, a voice I didn't have before.

I was connecting with people simply by sharing a little piece of my life, which made girls in the same situation feel not so alone. I wasn't going to let others decide for me what I would do with my life or what I would share. I wouldn't let the negativity drive me to build walls or live in fear of what people would say or think about me. Negative people can tear you down or propel you forward; it's really your choice how you'll let them affect you. Everyone has a voice and a story, but no one is going to hear yours if you don't speak up. It takes courage to be vulnerable and put yourself out there, but it's also very rewarding.

I'd been so unhappy and confused about what I was going to do with my life, while Harold was so busy and focused. So when the video went viral, it was like BOOM! *You can influence people right here and now, doing what you love.* I received hundreds of messages from girls who could relate to what I was thinking and feeling and who wanted me to make more videos.

I wasn't really thinking long term when I made my first video, and I hardly knew anything about how YouTube worked, but someone finally pointed out that people were subscribing to my YouTube channel. I didn't even notice until I had about a hundred subscribers.

Harold continued to support me when I decided to keep making videos. I probably would have stopped posting them if he had felt weird about it. Luckily, he didn't. His positive attitude and resistance to outside pressure were infectious. While he was supportive, his mind remained caught up in the challenge of the climb. (Yet, in the midst of it all, he surprised me with a cruise.*) So, I threw myself into my videos, many of which pertained to wedding updates, decor, invitations, items on our registry, and even my bridal showers.

* Watch our cruise video at Earls.org/cruise.

"There's some bad weather coming," I tell Rachel, who is currently in Colorado with her friend Hannah. "We want to be cautious, so we're going to climb down to Base Camp and rest for a few days to allow the storm to pass."

Rachel knows it will be a long climb down, but she says she's glad we'll be getting out of the storm and heading to a safer place. She doesn't sound worried. At least not yet.

Soon I feel the ferocious wind whipping my body back and forth as I cautiously step one foot in front of the other. For eight hours, I trek over jagged rocks and ice until my exhausted body finally arrives safely at Base Camp. After catching my breath, I look around to see that most of the other climbers have returned by now. I don't see Dave or Chad anywhere, and I'm starting to get concerned. I look at the time; it's 10:30 p.m.

They should be here by now.

I lean out of the mess tent and yell over to Dave's tent, "Dave! You over there?"

The air is crisp and getting colder by the minute. The temperature is well below freezing. It's pitch black outside with no moon. The trail above our camp resembles a dark alley, making it easy for climbers to take a wrong step. Are they injured? Sick? Maybe one of them got hurt and the other is with him or possibly going for help. Perhaps they headed over to the all-female Russian climbing team's mess tent to socialize.

After slipping on my unstrapped boots, I head out with

a couple of others from my team to the Russian climbers'
tents.

"Draswitcha, kak dela?" I greet them. "Have you seen
our friends Dave and Chad?"

"Nyet, we haven't seen them," they say.

Now I'm really nervous.

We check with the other international teams (the Chil-
eans, Mexicans, and Chinese), and nobody has heard or
seen anything. It's a courtesy on this part of the mountain
to keep an eye out for climbers in distress. Since we aren't
in the death zone yet, rescue is very possible. I try to rein
in my imagination. I don't want to think about what might
have happened. All I know is that I need to find them . . .
now. I begin hiking up the trail.

It's not long before my adrenaline is pumping, and I
begin a steady jog. My headlamp is on, but I still watch
the trail carefully, knowing how easy it would be to make a
dangerous misstep.

God, please help us find them.

# No Food, No Cake, No Condoms

**HAROLD**

It was late May in 2015, just under a year until the Everest expedition and less than a month until our wedding. After the excitement and celebration of my graduation and commissioning as an officer in the United States Army, it was time to pack up and leave the place I had just spent the past four years, a place filled with late-night studying, early-morning formations, and lots of self-growth.

I felt pride in my accomplishments, but the best feeling was piling all my stuff in the back of my family's Ford Expedition and pulling out of the gates with my arm around Rachel. I was smiling so big as we drove away from the Academy for the last time. Rachel and I were finally together and could kiss our long-distance relationship goodbye, for the time being at least.

If you added up all the days we'd actually spent together over the past two and a half years, it was something like ninety-eight days. It wasn't much. Even crazier, I proposed after spending only fifty-three days in person with Rachel!

Our wedding was just two weeks after graduation, and I made

sure those days were filled with quality face-to-face time to make up for the time apart. We went on hikes in the mountains and visited waterfalls, all while family members ran around frantically prepping for the wedding. I wasn't the slightest bit nervous about the wedding; I just wanted to be married already. I couldn't care less how the wedding looked as long as my bride was walking down the aisle. She could still be wearing that baggy camo T-shirt, and I'd be happy.

While I didn't put much thought into the wedding itself, I'd be lying if I didn't mention how excited I was when I thought about our wedding night. We had both waited to have sex for the past twenty-two years (Rachel had actually just turned twenty-three), although it was anything but easy. Our fierce attraction to each other, coupled with the strain of being able to see each other only about once a month, built up the moments when we were together with so much passion. But we consciously chose to hold back, as we had decided together to wait until we were married.

I think a lot of couples struggle with this, wondering, *Why should we wait if we know we are getting married?* We had this conversation one night as our feelings intensified. In the end, we leaned on the verse from 1 Corinthians 13:4 (NIV), which starts with "Love is patient." It goes on to describe what love is in a bunch of ways, but it stuck out to us that *patient* was the first word to describe love. We might have known we would get married, but we hadn't made that commitment to each other yet. So we chose to exercise our love for each other by being patient. Being on the other side now, I know it was a definite gift from God for us. Plus, waiting amped up the anticipation and made me want her even more. It was fun talking about our wedding night together.

To be clear, while waiting was the best decision we ever made, we didn't expect the first few times to be crazy magical, like in the movies. We had no idea what we were doing, but we had a lifetime to figure it out! And that's the fun in it. Exploring something for the first time together is fun in and of itself.

**RACHEL**

I can't emphasize enough how glad I am that we chose to wait. Before meeting Harold, I assumed by the time I found my person, he probably would have not waited. It was so encouraging when I learned Harold had made the same decision. It gave me confidence going into our marriage, knowing I'd never struggle with feelings of comparison.

We got married in Cashiers, North Carolina, at a country club overlooking an alpine lake with the Appalachian Mountains behind us. I thought for sure I'd be emotional when I woke up on our wedding day, June 11, 2015, but I was calm. One of my worst fears had always been that my dad, who turned seventy shortly before my wedding, was going to pass away before he could walk me down the aisle. His brother and sister both died from heart attacks at age forty-two, and his father died from cancer at sixty-four. Thankfully, my dad was alive and thriving. I was finally going to get to share that moment with him and dance to the song "Cinderella" by Steven Curtis Chapman for our father-daughter dance, like I had always dreamed.

That morning, I sent my maid of honor off to deliver a present for Harold that I had been working on over the years. I documented as much as I possibly could about our relationship and combined everything into a big memorabilia scrapbook so that we could always remember the stories that brought us together. I included printed Facebook messages and texts, our snail mail, and little items from our dates and wrote down all the details. That scrapbook had it all. Even the screenshot from our very first phone call.

When it was time for the ceremony, all our friends and family were seated outside under a white tent with the most gorgeous view of the mountains in the background. There was a long stone pathway from the lawn up to the country club, where all my bridesmaids were lined up and waiting inside behind the glass doors, with my dad and me at the very end. As the music started, each one left for the long walk down the aisle.

After my maid of honor started her walk, it was just my dad and me standing together. He was the man who had my heart from the very beginning. He held me when I was born, watched me take my first steps, and held my hand as I stepped on his toes while we danced together. This was the moment I'd dreamed about since I was a little girl. That's when every emotion hit me. He held out his arm, and I took it. I had been his little girl my entire life. His spit-firey, curly-haired, redheaded little soccer champ was now a strong, confident woman ready to take on the world with the love of her life. Tears streamed down my face the whole way down the aisle, only increasing as my view of Harold got better. We locked eyes with so much love beaming out of us. I'm pretty sure our entire family was crying.

The song "A Thousand Years" was playing, and I successfully made it down the aisle without tripping on my dress or fainting. But when I looked at Harold, I saw his whole body was tense. I'd never seen him so emotional. I couldn't even focus on what the pastor was saying because I glanced down and saw that Harold's fingers were clenched into fists. I looked into his eyes and thought, *Are you okay?*

## HAROLD

I told all my groomsmen that I didn't think I'd cry. I thought I'd just be really happy and smile a lot. Plus, I'd never cried in public before. I respect men who are connected with their emotional sides; I just didn't think that was me. Then I saw the double doors swing open, and Rachel started coming down the aisle. To my surprise, she wasn't wearing an extra-large camo T-shirt but an elegant long white fitted dress with lace. Her long, curly red hair was lit up from the sun setting behind her. Her green eyes locked on mine as her father held her hand. Tears started streaming down her cute freck-led face as her smile broke through despite her intense emotions.

I lost it. I immediately started crying. Like sobbing. Like awkward tears, where everyone stops looking at the bride and turns to look at the groom. It was a long walk, and I cried, then dried up, then cried again and again. It was so intense watching my beautiful bride walk down the aisle and realizing she was finally mine and I was hers. The emotions inside became so overwhelming that my body went into total lockdown. It was almost like I had a seizure, and that's not an exaggeration.

I was having second thoughts about getting married. Just kidding! I seriously couldn't feel my fingers at all; everything was tingling. Rachel grabbed my fingers to try to help me relax, but when the pastor said to hold the candle, I realized I couldn't open my fingers because they were so tightly clenched. This had never happened to me. All I could think about besides Rachel was trying to feel my hands and make my body look normal. Some of our wedding pictures are hilarious because you can see that my face and hands are super intense and pale.

I somehow figured out how to relax toward the end of the ceremony. I kept bending my knees, practically jumping up and down, because I just wanted to kiss her!*

After the ceremony, we went into the reception cheering, with our arms raised and the biggest smiles on our faces. We were ready to cut loose, celebrate, and crush it on the dance floor! Rachel is a dancing champ: she can salsa, slow dance, waltz, twerk, whip, nae nae, dougie, stanky leg, dab, or dab into a stanky leg. You name it, she can do it! Meanwhile, I can snap my fingers like in the movie *Hitch*.

When it was time for the toasts, Rachel's dad, who is certainly the quiet and less chatty parent, surprised everyone with a toast we'd look back on and laugh about for years to come. Well, maybe I shouldn't call it a toast. That thing was a novel. He compared

* Watch our wedding video at Earls.org/wedding.

Rachel to an Arabian horse at one point. It was hard to hear him because he held the mic too far from his mouth, but he seemed to enjoy himself. He told everybody that Rachel's mom never let him talk and this was his moment, so he took it!

For our last dance, we had the DJ play "Let's Get It On" by Marvin Gaye. We thought it was hilarious and the perfect way to start off our wedding night. But first, we needed to find some food. We were starving because we had been so busy at the reception talking to everyone that we didn't get a bite to eat. Actually, I think I had one bite of cake, but Rachel smeared most of it on my face. Someone (the best man) was supposed to pack us some food to go, but he forgot. Not to name names, but Tommy Ferguson was my best man. We were also exhausted, but none of that really mattered because we were excited to enjoy our wedding night.

My groomsmen were supposed to square me away with everything for the wedding night (*cough, cough:* condoms), but Tommy came up and said, "We totally forgot to get your stuff, man."

No food. No cake. And now no condoms.

No problem. We'd go find what we needed.

We started driving around North Carolina late at night, but Cashiers is a mountain town, and everything closes at five o'clock. Nothing was open, not even a drugstore or gas station. After about an hour of aimlessly driving, we finally found an open gas station with bars on the windows perched on a street corner, but they were out of condoms.

We didn't find another open place, so we headed to our hotel and decided to take our chances. People were already making bets on when we'd get pregnant; lots of them thought we'd have a honeymoon baby. While we did want to wait a little bit before having kids, we'd also be over the moon whenever God brought a little blessing into our lives.

Where is everybody?

Tommy left just before me, and he must have been booking it too since I can't see or hear any sign of him. I speed up to a fast jog and soon spot a couple of headlamps ahead.

"Chad? Dave?" I call out. No answer.

I estimate the light is about a half mile away, so I keep up my pace. A few moments later, the light veers off the trail in a different direction. I know there's another camp over there, so it can't be them. About ten minutes later, I spot a cluster of three headlamps again on the trail.

"Tommy? Is that you?" I call out into the dark.

I start running hard. I'm praying hard too. The steepest part of the trail has an eighty-degree slope to the left. If you take a wrong step, you can fall close to a hundred feet down into the rocks. Although it's difficult to see anything clearly in the dark, I think I can make out two people huddled over a third figure lying on the ground. It must be them.

"Hey, Tommy, is that you?" I call up the trail as I slow down. "This is Harold. Is that Dave?"

"Yes, it's Dave."

I'm still about five hundred feet away, so it's hard to hear Tommy yelling.

I start to realize Chad, the combat-wounded amputee of the team, isn't with them and something is seriously wrong with Dave, our seasoned climber and team doctor. Has Chad gone on ahead? Have I missed him? Could he still be out here somewhere?

As I get closer, I can hear better, so I continue asking questions. A Russian doctor is with them. Tommy tells me Dave has High Altitude Pulmonary Edema (HAPE), a serious type of altitude sickness. He is weak, confused, and needs help.

"He's in bad shape," Tommy says.

# An Extra Seventeen Swiss Francs
# for the Funeral

## HAROLD

One dream Rachel and I shared was to see and experience as much of the world as possible. So naturally when it came time to plan our honeymoon, we were on the same page: we wanted a grand adventure, exploring as many new places as we could. Our first stop was Spain. The morning after our wedding, we drove four-plus hours to Charleston, South Carolina, to catch a military plane.

The military has an excellent benefit: if you're active duty, you and your dependents can fly on a military plane for free, under certain circumstances. While we were a little tired, we were excited for the adventure ahead and the uninterrupted time we'd have together. We walked out onto the tarmac and saw the massive C-17 military cargo plane pull up.

"That looks like it could eat a normal-sized plane!" Rachel said.

After the pilot lowered the door and we climbed in, we sat in the seats located on either side of the plane facing inward. The seats were somewhat comfortable, and they even gave us small blankets!

"What's in those huge pallets?" Rachel asked, pointing to the cargo in the middle of the plane. "They look like missiles."

I laughed. "Those are just helicopter parts."

## RACHEL

Well, they looked like missiles to me. The seven-hour flight was loud and freezing cold. The seats were tiny and stiff. But I was so exhausted I ended up lying down on the floor curled under my jacket and sleeping most of the way, noise and all. When I woke up, we had landed in Rota, Spain. Somehow we missed getting our passports stamped. Apparently, we were supposed to go to a police station to do that, but no one told us. It didn't seem like a big deal at the time, but as we soon would find out, it put us in a scary predicament.

We hit the ground running, and we roughed it hard-core. Seventeen countries in thirty days. We loved every minute of it. Our honeymoon adventure was a testament that money doesn't buy you happiness. But time together and new experiences do! Nothing we did was luxurious, but everything we did was memorable. We stayed in hostels, engaging with the people around us, never really knowing where we'd end up. Positive memories you can look back on have more longevity than material objects, which will quickly lose your affection.

Knowing this, I filmed our whole adventure to capture our memories. Every night, as Harold would get on his phone and do research to find our next destination, I would edit the footage and post videos of the day on my YouTube channel. We slowly started gaining viewers from around the world. An article about us was even published in Slovakia after they saw our video. I'm not sure what it said, though, because it was written in Slovak.*

When we were in Switzerland, we decided to go paragliding. A girl who worked at the hostel we were staying at recommended a small company run by her dad and told us she was in training to

* Watch our entire trip at Earls.org/honeymoon.

become certified. We were trusting and thought we were getting a great deal, saving seventeen Swiss francs and avoiding the high-traffic tourist spots. Two men were our guides. One was a seasoned paraglider decked out in professional gear, including a nice helmet and a GoPro camera. The second guy wore what looked like a bicycle helmet, elbow pads, and a camera duct-taped to a pole.

## HAROLD

Obviously, I chose the first guy with the brand-new equipment. Rachel gave me a look of complete shock that I was happily entrusting my new bride to a guy with sketchy gear. But honestly, I didn't think twice about it. Clearly, I had a lot to learn about marriage!

The girl from the hostel went first. She put her gear on and started running across the top of the mountain. As she approached the ledge, she started to jump, trying to catch flight, but when she was about six feet in the air, she nose-dived into the ground about fifty feet from the ledge. My immediate response was "Uhhhhh-hh . . . is this safe to do?" My life started flashing in front of my eyes, but I gained some confidence when I looked over at Rachel's janky gear, most of which looked homemade. *Glad I'm not in Rachel's shoes*, I thought after seeing what had just happened.

I pictured the coyote from the cartoon *Looney Tunes* running off the cliff, pedaling his feet in midair as fast as he could and then falling straight down like a rock. That's all, folks.

"Totally fine," my guy said in his Swiss accent. "No worries at all. She is still in training. Just run off the cliff, and the wind takes it from there."

That's when I regretted letting Rachel go with the other guy, as well as taking the cheaper paragliding service just to save a few bucks. *At least if one of us dies, we'll have an extra seventeen Swiss francs for the funeral.*

Rachel went first, taking off in a full sprint for the edge of the mountain and then soaring into the air. Turns out her guy was a pro, just with semipro gear. I had taken her phone so I could shoot some video, even though she was reluctant to let me use it.

"I promise I won't drop it," I said to Rachel, waving her phone as I took off after her.

While my guide and I were running across the bumpy ground and about to lift off, the phone fell out of my pants pocket and hit the ground. It started flipping end over end. I knew if it fell over the edge, we were never going to see it again. I'd certainly have some explaining to do, and all our honeymoon video footage and photos would be lost. I still don't know how, but I reached down and grabbed it while on the run, right before I launched out over a three-thousand-foot drop.

## RACHEL

Semipro gear? Ha! He looked more like a kid riding his bike for the first time. I'm sure as they read this right now, my mom and dad are super thrilled with Harold for leaving me with Mr. Semipro! Actually, I 100 percent know that my mom is blowing up his phone while she says to my dad, "Billllll! You're not going to believe this!"

The Lord must have been looking out for Harold, because I probably would have made him go on a ridiculous hunt through the mountains looking for my phone had he dropped it!

Paragliding in Switzerland will go down as one of the more epic parts of our honeymoon, janky gear and all. Another memorable adventure was hitchhiking across Greece. It started when we thought the cheapest way to get from Italy to Greece was by taking a big, rickety, empty, old cargo ship. It looked like a cruise ship from the outside, so I thought, *Oh, this will be fun*. It was the furthest thing from fun! It was packed with truckers who'd driven their 18-wheelers onto the ship. There was nothing to do, and no one had a private room. The ship had a small common room full of what looked like old airplane seats arranged in rows, and that was where we were supposed to stay. It was sketchy as all get out!

## HAROLD

There was one guy who was a little different, though. His name was Gerry, and he was well dressed in a dark blue cardigan sweater. We gravitated toward him, and I struck up a conversation. I found out he had business interests in Italy and Russia and owned a "small" villa in Greece, where he was currently transporting one of his cars. I talked to him for hours while the ship crossed from Lecce, Italy, to Athens, Greece. Gerry said he was planning to get off the ship one stop earlier than we were.

"Where are you planning to go?" he asked.

"Eventually Istanbul, but we might stop in Athens," I said.

"Hey, why don't you ride with me to the villa? We're right on the beach. It's not far from Istanbul. You can take a bus from there."

It seems strange now to plan a ride across Greece with a complete stranger during our honeymoon, but it made sense at the time. Plus, Rachel was beyond ready to get off that ship! Soon we were in Gerry's car, bumping along rural roads. I was sharing life stories and practically becoming best friends with him, while Rachel sprawled out in the back seat, catching up on the lack of sleep from the boat ride. I think she slept the entire eight-hour drive.

We were in Greece for only two days before we hopped on a bus headed to Turkey. After a few hours, the bus stopped, so we all passed up our passports to get stamped as we crossed over the border. Or so we thought. A few minutes later, we heard a man at the front of the bus say, "I need the two Americans." Rachel and I looked at each other and started to panic. We knew we were only about three hundred miles from the Syrian border and that our situation had the potential to go south if they found out I was in the US military.

The movie *Taken* flashed through my head. We reluctantly stood up, grabbed our backpacks, and headed toward the front of the bus while everyone stared at us. A customs officer led us inside the border security facility and made us wait in the hallway. We sat there for forty minutes. No one would talk to us. Then two officers pulled us into an interrogation room with a metal table and what looked like a two-way mirror. One of them said, "How did you get here?"

We tried to explain, but the questions kept coming, rapid fire.

"How long have you been here? You don't have any paperwork. How did you get into Europe?"

Finally, we realized the problem: we were trying to leave the European Union without stamps in our passports from landing in Spain. So, in their eyes, we weren't even officially there.

## RACHEL

It wasn't an interrogation room. It was more of an office with a table, chairs, and some papers. I kept trying to tell them I could show them video footage on my phone of every single day of our trip, but they weren't interested. They were very suspicious and wanted documented proof of how we'd gotten into the EU with no passport stamp. I found a receipt and showed them a video of us getting on the plane. Our bus driver then came in and threatened to leave us because he had been waiting for so long. Thankfully, Harold was not about to let him leave us in the middle of nowhere and very sternly told him, "You will not leave." So he waited.

Finally, after enough charades and their good cop/bad cop routine, they released us. We got back on the bus and rolled into Turkey, only to discover we had arrived during the busy Ramadan holiday. We deeply appreciated every cultural experience, and so did our viewers. I received lots of comments about how people felt like they were on this journey with us and were thankful we were sharing.

Our honeymoon was far from typical, but the experiences we shared are priceless. The most memorable moments aren't the times we spent the extra money for a taxi or ate at a nice restaurant. They're the times when life didn't go as planned. It was during these times that we learned the importance of being a team. It's the not-so-perfect moments that teach you to lean on each other, laugh together despite the circumstances, and navigate unforeseen challenges. I watched Harold step up in a bunch of ways. While we were going from one unfamiliar place to another, he always took the lead, and my trust in him grew.

We'd made our way through seventeen countries and were finally back home. But the adventure hadn't ended. I noticed our first day back that my period was two months late. "Holy smokes!" This was not normal for me, so we anxiously headed to Target to buy a pregnancy test.

We both had mixed feelings. If I were pregnant, we'd have a baby by the time Harold left for his Everest expedition and I'd be alone as a new mom while he climbed the highest mountain in the world. It was a strange feeling. I went to the bathroom inside Target, did what needed to be done, quickly shoved the test back into the box without looking at it, and headed back to the car.

We sat in our car in the middle of the Target parking lot, staring at the pregnancy test. What was it going to be? We held our breath and waited.

## HAROLD

In true Rachel fashion, she took out her phone and started recording as we each looked at the results of the pregnancy test. This was the first pregnancy test she had ever taken, and neither of us knew how to read it properly.

"Is it supposed to be one line or two?" I asked, leaning over the center console to Rachel's side of the car.

I'm not sure why we didn't just buy the one that said "pregnant" or "not pregnant." That would have been easier. We were both feeling anxious. I wasn't sure what I was hoping for.

Only one line appeared, which meant we were not pregnant.

We were mostly relieved, but the possibility of being pregnant stirred up so many emotions, and we were starting to get used to the idea of possibly having a baby soon. It wasn't surprising that our crazy monthlong backpacking, hitchhiking, scuba-diving honeymoon adventure probably led to Rachel's period being thrown all out of whack.

We couldn't wait to start a family, but according to the pregnancy test, it looked like we'd be waiting a little longer.

I see Tommy and the Russian doctor talking to Dave and checking his vitals. They're trying to determine if he can walk back to camp if we help him. Dave slurs his words and appears disoriented, almost like he's in a drunken state.

"Where's Chad?" I ask.

"Dave says he went ahead to get help."

Dave is an intelligent and highly skilled climber. He's someone I look up to for his knowledge and climbing experience. Seeing that something like this can happen to one of our best, at a relatively simple part of the climb, is eye opening for me.

We still need to find Chad.

Since I didn't pass him and he's not in our camp, he must be out here somewhere. Is he suffering from HAPE too? Is he injured? Does he have a problem with his prosthesis? Maybe it malfunctioned or got damaged.

A couple of Russians arrive with oxygen for Dave, and together we get him moving toward our camp. After carefully walking with Dave arm in arm across the frozen, rocky path leading back to Base Camp, we settle in the mess tent. I watch the Russian treat Dave with oxygen, hydration, and some Kit Kat bars. He can barely sit up and is acting loopy, like he's not all there.

A figure walks into the tent and greets us. "Well, hey, guys," Chad says.

He had gone to another camp near the trail to try to get

help. The amputated nub on his leg is bruised badly from all the extra walking as he sought help for Dave. When Dave started getting sick, they slowed down. Soon Dave could barely walk as exhaustion set in and the temperature dropped. Chad was a hero, carrying both packs—his own on his back and Dave's on his front—while going ahead to get help.

We bond in the mess tent this night, taking care of Dave and trying to cheer him up. The team rallied when we realized guys were in trouble. We perform better when we know a team has our back. No one hesitated to sprint into that cold, dark, dangerous night to find our two missing teammates. Would Dave have made it back to camp without help? I don't know. I feel honored to be part of a team like this.

We quickly learn that one of our biggest challenges is keeping the team together while we are climbing, due to the harsh conditions and everyone's unique climbing pace. I don't like the feeling of being separated from any of the team members. Since I came up with the idea for the expedition and helped start USX, I feel responsible.

We try to fix this problem by redistributing weight among one another's packs to slow down the faster climbers and speed up the slower ones. It works! For a couple of hours, at least. We also pair up into buddy teams based on climbing speeds.*

* What is blatantly obvious now, that I wish we'd known then, is that it is better to climb as a team than to split into buddy pairs. In pairs, more things can go wrong and there are fewer people to help. Sadly, our failure to stick together as a team put us in an extremely dangerous and costly situation later on the mountain.

# 11

# That Could Have Been Me

**HAROLD**

I was so caught up in planning our epic honeymoon that I didn't exactly have a plan for where we'd be living when we got back. Although I had graduated, I was going to be stationed at West Point for another four to six months so I could fully recover from my shoulder surgery.

After we flew back to the States, we made our way across the parking lot to our car. We'd left it in long-term parking, and it was filled to the roof with all our wedding gifts, almost exclusively for the kitchen. Rachel and I burst out laughing when we saw the car, forgetting how packed it really was. There was a blender, a complete china set, and a bunch of new bath towels pressed up against the window. To this day, our bath towels have sun-stained brownish-yellow marks from being pressed against the window for thirty-five days!

We began our twelve-hour drive to Highland Falls, New York, with no furniture and no apartment to go to. On the drive up, we were trying to look up places to live, but we weren't having any luck.

When we were about two hours outside New York, we found a Realtor online who told us she had a perfect place for us. We said we'd take it, sight unseen. We didn't even look at the pictures. We signed the contract in a McDonald's parking lot at 10:30 p.m., as soon as we arrived in Highland Falls.

We didn't know it at the time, but our 467-square-foot apartment was a former carriage house owned by J. P. Morgan, a famous banker who once owned a huge estate in the area. While the horses and other four-legged friends were long gone, the eight-legged critters had taken up residence. Without any furniture, they were easy to see as they crept about on their long legs, making audible crunches when we stepped on them.

We didn't waste any time hopping on Craigslist to find some stuff for our tiny apartment. Somehow, we ended up looking at furniture in a $2 million mansion. We had rented a U-Haul to pick up a couch and a bookcase, but once we arrived, the family told us they were moving and wanted to get rid of a bunch of stuff.

"Anything you want you can have," they told us. Rachel and I looked at each other with wide eyes like, *You say whaaaaat!?!?* It was such a God thing. He kept providing when we had nothing. We ended up leaving with the couch and bookcase, plus a bedroom set, end tables, gold-rimmed mirrors, a mattress set, a table, and chairs. And they didn't charge us for anything! We took so much of their furniture that our U-Haul was completely full, so the man gave us the keys to his trailer. We hitched it to the back of the U-Haul, and he asked that we just drop it off at his brother's house after we'd unpacked. Then he asked if I'd ever towed a trailer before.

"Yeah, of course!" I said.

I'd never driven a trailer in my life, but I wasn't going to admit that, absolutely not. All men instinctively know how to drive with a trailer attached. It comes naturally to us. Just spin the wheel this way, then swing it back, and voilà! Too easy.

Once the furniture was loaded, I started to back down, and we waved goodbye to their entire family standing at the top of the driveway. I turned the wheel this way, then swung it back. Immediately the trailer started to go off the driveway. I pulled forward and tried again. I spent twenty minutes trying to get out of the driveway.

The kind man came up to me after the sixth attempt. "You want some help?"

"Nah, I'm good," I said as Rachel covered her face with her hands trying to hide her smile. "The steering wheel is being a little figgity, that's all."

All the while, Rachel was coaching me from the passenger seat like she was a grand master trailer operator and pit crew chief. We eventually got out of that complicated driveway, and to this day there are probably tire tracks in that yard. I bet they had to plant a garden to cover up the ruts. Good thing they were moving.

**RACHEL**

The unexpected generosity of total strangers almost made up for the tiny apartment with no dishwasher, no washing machine and dryer, and all the bugs. At least we had a real bed now! I love looking back at where we started because everything we built together was from the ground up and due to the generosity of others. I've learned that generosity produces joy on all fronts. There is joy in giving, knowing you're helping someone. Joy is also felt when you're on the receiving end, knowing someone cares enough about you to help.

A few months later, when Harold's recovery time at West Point was over, we moved on post at Fort Benning, Georgia, where Harold was stationed.

We felt like royalty walking into our 950-square-foot apartment! Our new home was double the size of our last home, which meant we definitely did not have enough furniture to fill it. Luckily, we were only about two and a half hours from Harold's family, and they gave us some of their old furniture to help fill it up.

Harold's grandma (Ganga, as we call her) had a basement that looked like an antique furniture thrift store, and she basically let me go wild. She had everything from unused oven mitts to mounted deer heads, and she usually had two of each item. She would pick up random things and ask me if we wanted them. The best of all was an old washing machine that still worked.

"We'll take it," I said with enthusiasm.

It sure beat driving to the laundromat and always needing quarters on hand to wash our clothes. We brought that baby home and found it came with a nice surprise inside: a dead rat! I can't help but laugh thinking about how cheap we were. We could have bought ourselves a new washer, but I'm so low maintenance that the rodent didn't bother me too much.

I must admit having a washing machine did make things easier, once the rat and dead rat smell were gone. We still didn't have a dryer, though, so I'd hang our laundry to dry in the bathroom. We made do with what we had and were always more than happy.

We've become experts at finding new and creative ways to have fun that don't cost any money, like playing air hockey on the upside-down kitchen table, although there wasn't any air. (I crushed Harold, by the way). For our first New Year's Eve together, we didn't get all fancy and go to a party that had fireworks. Instead, we wore our sweatpants, covered our faces in one-dollar exfoliating face masks, set up our cornhole in the hallway, and drank out of our crystal wedding goblets that one of my mom's friends had given us. We didn't have much, but we knew how to have fun with what we had.

It wasn't long before Harold's military training picked up and he was gone a lot, which meant I had a lot of lonely nights. I really wanted to get a dog to keep me company, so I came up with my best sales pitch, trying to convince Harold it was a good idea.

I did my research and found what I thought would be the perfect dog for us: an Australian shepherd. We brought adorable six-week-old Ranger home in January. A month later, while Harold was away for a week, I couldn't sleep one night and randomly came across an Australian cattle dog puppy for sale on Craigslist. My dog when I was growing up, Boomerang, who still lives with my parents, is an Australian cattle dog, and he is the best. I messaged the lady and drove there the next day to see the dog. It was love at first sight. I couldn't get ahold of Harold, so I brought the puppy home and named her Tracker. A few days later, Harold finally called and said, "I can't wait to get home. What are you up to right now?"

"Taking out the puppiesssss," I said.

I was a tiny bit nervous to hear his reaction. He certainly wasn't enthusiastic, nor was he upset; he was simply indifferent. In my defense, we had talked about getting a second dog so that Ranger would have a friend to play with. They already felt like my children, and having them with me during Harold's frequent absences was a game changer.

At the beginning of February 2016, about two months before Harold would leave for Everest, we decided to start actively trying for a baby. We'd been going back and forth on whether we should wait until after he got back. Harold really wanted me to be pregnant before he left in case he didn't make it back. He said he wanted me to have a part of him with me, no matter what happened.

It wasn't as clear for me. I was struggling with the possibility of getting pregnant before Everest because of all the unknowns. Since the first trimester is the scary zone, with the highest possibility of a miscarriage, I thought about how hard it would be if I had a miscarriage right before he left for Everest. Or while he was on Everest. The weight of the pain from losing my baby would be unbearable to begin with, and the thought of having to go through that traumatic experience by myself was unsettling. Plus, Harold would be going through the loss too, which would be distracting and emotional when he should have his full focus on Everest.

Instead of being able to live with the excitement of possibly getting pregnant, every terrifying scenario ran through my head on repeat. If I did get pregnant and, God forbid, something went wrong on Everest resulting in Harold's death, I'd instantly become a single parent with no stable job to support our child and no father to love him the way I knew Harold would.

Maybe the most terrifying scenario would be if I didn't get pregnant before Everest and Harold didn't make it back. I would never get to have kids with the love of my life, the one thing I wanted more than anything. I'd never get to look at my child and notice all the little ways he resembles Harold, like the way Harold's face lights up when he smiles, or his crazy wild personality, or his tender heart and the way he loves to snuggle more than anything. I wouldn't get to tell our child stories of his incredible father and the way he fiercely loved me and made me laugh all the time. I wouldn't get to do any of those things because our family wouldn't exist if Harold didn't make it back.

The movie *Everest* had recently come out. The film is based on Jon Krakauer's book *Into Thin Air*, which is about the deadly day on Everest that killed Rob Hall and several others. Harold's father called him one day and told him he'd just finished watching the movie. He then warned him not to watch it with me because it was intense. Especially given the reality of Everest being just around the corner for us.

We were in the car when Harold's dad called, and the phone was on speaker. I had been reading *Into Thin Air* just to gain some general knowledge of Everest, so I quickly put it down. I had no plans to watch the movie either. I had enough of my own fears already, and reading or watching terrifying events taking place on Everest would only make things worse. I certainly wasn't naive; I just knew I couldn't remain strong and supportive of my husband if I allowed my fears to take over.

## HAROLD

I, on the other hand, went online and started reading articles about it. I found an article from Jan Arnold, Rob Hall's widowed wife.

What I read was interesting, especially as we grappled with the decision of whether to try to get pregnant. As it turned out, Jan and Rob got pregnant with a baby girl right before he left for his Everest expedition. Jan described the last conversations she had with Rob when he called from a satellite phone as he was stuck near the summit. "I willed him to move, to try to get himself down the mountain, but I accepted he just couldn't."

As I read, I was in tears, knowing this conversation was one Rachel and I could be having in just a few short months. And, like Jan, Rachel could be pregnant. What confirmed my desire to get pregnant, however, was what Jan said toward the end of the interview, addressing how she coped with Rob's death: "For some weeks, I didn't feel alone, as I had his baby daughter inside me, moving even. I found those movements comforting."*

## RACHEL

Wow. Yep, I'm in tears. It's been four years since I lived those fearful moments, and that story just brings it all back. I could feel myself in her exact situation. That could have been me.

It's painful to revisit these emotions. I knew that even experienced climbers don't always make it back alive, so the odds might be even worse for Harold. I had no control over what might happen to my husband or my future.

As I thought about the risk, the worry felt overwhelming, and I turned to God. I couldn't pray only for Harold's safety; I had to pray also that God would carry me through this, no matter the outcome. That meant I had to fully put my faith in God.

If the worst were to happen and I lost my husband, whom I had only just begun to share my life with, somehow I would survive

---

* Shanee Edwards, *Everest:* Rob Hall's Wife Jan Arnold Shares Her Story of Loss and Fear, SheKnows, January 26, 2016, www.sheknows.com/entertainment/articles/1109945/interview-jan-arnold-rob-halls-wife-everest.

with God's support. If we did end up having a baby and my husband wasn't around to throw him up in the air, pretending he was a rocket ship, or chase him all around the house as he squealed at the top of his lungs, running and flailing his arms . . . If Harold missed his son's first word, which would have been *Daddy* had Harold been here . . . If he never got to witness the pure joy our son felt each time he saw a plane or school bus and then ran into my arms to get a better look . . .

I prayed that if Harold wasn't here for all those things, I would be able to be what our child needed. That I could somehow fill Harold's shoes and bring out the same amount of laughter and joy as Harold would have. I could never replace what would be lost, but I needed to put my faith in God that at the end of the day, we'd be okay.

I knew if the worst were to happen, it would be a long time before I'd be okay again. I wouldn't be the same, and the grief I would carry would probably never really heal with time. So I needed to trust that God would carry me, because it would take time and perseverance and a strength I knew I would not have on my own to get back on my feet after something like that.

I knew losing Harold would break me to the core. Just praying for his safety wasn't enough.

## May 7, 2016

Being on this mountain reminds me of the deadly events and harrowing news stories I've read over the last two years. At this point, 296 out of over 4,000 people have died while attempting to climb Everest. In 2014, 16 people were killed in a sudden avalanche at Base Camp. About a year later, 19 people died at Base Camp after a 7.8 earthquake triggered another deadly avalanche. As a result, the mountain was closed down by the Chinese government and there were no summits in 2015.

I can't help thinking about the avalanche on Everest in April 2014. I specifically remember learning about Menuka Magar-Gurung, the twenty-five-year-old wife of a Sherpa who had been among the 16 killed on that tragic day. She told the BBC, "I still feel he's alive" as she tried not to cry. In her arms, she held their ten-month-old son, Anish.

Then I remember Anita Lama, a twenty-three-year-old who was widowed on the same day, talking to the BBC while carrying her eleven-month-old daughter. "I never thought that such a tragedy would happen," she said as tears filled her eyes.*

After seeing this report, my eyes had grown red with tears. The eerie similarity in ages and stages of life between these women and Rachel terrifies me now. I had been given a raw and unfiltered look of what I very well could put

* Surendra Phuyal, "Sherpa Families' Sorrow After Killer Everest Avalanche," *BBC News*, May 8, 2014, www.bbc.com/news/world-asia-27316009.

Rachel through. The tragic events were described as the most deadly day in modern mountaineering. How Rachel supported me after these devastating avalanches, I'll never know.

We talk on the phone tonight at Base Camp under the moonlight and the watchful eye of Everest, but I decide not to share with Rachel the stories of sorrow that have been plaguing my mind.

Hearing her sweet, caring voice breaks me, and I can't help but picture her as the next grieving widow on the news.

# 12

# The Dirty Truth of Achieving Big Dreams

**RACHEL**

When we got back from our honeymoon, I started vlogging my daily life. Sometimes I'd include Harold (who was still slightly uncomfortable talking to a camera), but it was always through my lens. I had just reached one thousand subscribers.

Naturally, when Harold needed assistance with social media and began to increase fundraising efforts for the Everest expedition, I stepped in to help. I created and edited promotional photos and videos highlighting our cause of raising awareness for PTSD and Soldier suicide, started establishing a social media presence, and coordinated our efforts with our publicist, Amy.

Every good team needs a strong team name, so Harold and I gave ourselves the name Team Hungry. The story behind the name stems from our honeymoon while we were in Naples, Italy. After a long day visiting Pompeii, Harold and I had just gotten off our train and decided to walk back to our hotel. We could have easily taken a taxi for fewer than the seventeen francs we saved from paragliding, but we decided we should save the money.

It turned out to be an hour-long walk in blistering heat. We were so thirsty, and I kept singing, "I'm so hungry! I'm so hungry!" over and over again. A little while later, Harold's stomach started gurgling, making me laugh so hard. That's when I said, "We're Team Hungry," and it stuck.

It may sound silly that we call ourselves Team Hungry, but it reminds us that we're in it together. When we're going through the ups and downs of life, I can always look over and see my best friend fighting every battle with me. I highly encourage couples to come up with a team name, preferably something that will make you laugh during the tougher moments.

If you've ever been part of any kind of team, I'm sure you've experienced a time when not everyone got along. Maybe a team-mate made a bad move, didn't give it her all, didn't show up, or just started needless drama. The way forward is to refocus and realize you're on the same team.

I know I am better when Harold is on my team, and vice versa. We balance each other, show up for each other, and fight for each other. Together we are stronger. Tangible ways I show Harold I'm on his side include encouraging him, praying for him, and never leaving him to tackle his challenges alone. I try to take the initiative and find ways to be helpful, offer insight, or brainstorm new ideas.

We have a better chance of reaching our goals when we use our unique set of gifts to help each other, and ultimately there is no one I'd rather celebrate every victory with than Harold. If we lose, at least we lose together and cheer each other up over some Moose Tracks ice cream and half-baked chocolate chip cookies.

As teammates, Harold and I discussed my joining the team at Everest Base Camp to coordinate all the media and relay information back to Amy while on the mountain. Ultimately, we decided against it.

## HAROLD

I had two big concerns about Rachel coming to Base Camp. First,

I knew I'd be worried about her safety. There would be a steady stream of people flowing through the tent city from all over the world. This came with its own dangers, including leaving her alone with strangers in China. What if they found out I was in the US military? Would they question Rachel?

Plus, altitude sickness is common there, as are some nasty stomach bugs. There was just too much uncertainty, which meant I would be thinking about her safety when I needed to be fully focused on the mission. Loss of focus could mean loss of life.

I also worried about what it would be like for her if something did happen to me up on the mountain. She'd be right there at Base Camp, hearing the play-by-play on the communications systems but being unable to do anything about it. I could literally be dying on the mountain above her, and she'd have no way to get to me. At least if she was at home on the other side of the world, there would be some space between us, and being surrounded by friends and family might make it a little bit easier if something bad happened.

Early on, we realized we needed a Base Camp manager to communicate events on the mountain to our stateside publicist, social media coordinator, and the national media. The Base Camp manager would also help Dave with filming the documentary we had planned to make to continue raising awareness for our cause.

I had reached out to several veterans about being a Base Camp manager but had no success. After briefly contemplating and then dismissing the idea of having Rachel come, I approached one of the first people I told about my Everest quest: Tommy.

Though Tommy was my best friend, that wasn't why I asked him to be Base Camp manager. Originally, I had no intention of asking him to take part, but I didn't know anyone else who could be available for this important role for two months. It just made sense from a financial and operations perspective.

It wasn't until four months before departing that I asked Tommy if he would be interested in going. I'm surprised his wife, Tati, let him go. At that point in their marriage, he'd never spent a night away from her! Tommy confirmed his company would give him the necessary time off. Not only that, but they would donate $5,000 to the cause, and he would receive $3,000 from his brother-in-law's company, more than covering the cost for him to join the team.

Two months prior to leaving for our expedition, our team experienced a crushing blow. Since our first phone call a little over a year earlier, CPT Matt Hickey was supposed to be our expedition leader. He had a breadth of mountaineering leadership experience, and he was the current commander at the US Army World Class Athlete Program, which was responsible for training Soldiers participating in the Olympics.

Unexpectedly, he was informed by his commanding general that he wouldn't be allowed to climb, given his duties with the upcoming Olympics. Our team had a conference call immediately following the news. We talked seriously about canceling the expedition but ultimately decided we would climb anyway, without an expedition leader.

Although we wouldn't have an actual leader on the mountain, the rest of the team had extensive climbing experience. Except me! We didn't know it at the time, but the lack of a climbing leader would put all our lives at risk while we were on the mountain.

Rachel was particularly uneasy after learning that Matt would be unable to come and that we still planned on climbing. She saw Matt as added security for me. He had trained me how to climb on ice and kept me under his wing over the past year. Now he wasn't going to be there to keep me safe.

**RACHEL**

Added security? I think he means the *only* security! Matt was the most knowledgeable about Everest, so losing him as the team leader worried me. I didn't want more things to fall on Harold's shoulders. He had more than enough to handle bringing awareness to their

PTSD cause, and, quite frankly, I wasn't too confident in his climbing knowledge or experience.

One time we went rock climbing together, and Harold helped me put on my harness. When I came down and expressed how painful it felt, we realized I was wearing it like a thong instead of like a seat, which is the proper way!

It was now just days before Harold was to leave for Everest on April 7, 2016. He had started packing his gear for his two-month Everest adventure, but nothing was guaranteed. There were still hurdles to overcome. For starters, Everest had been closed to climbing expeditions for more than two years after two consecutive climbing seasons had left thirty-five people dead. Just to put things into perspective, the highest number of deaths to occur on Everest happened in those two years. Naturally, you'd think the death rate would be lower now since technology has advanced so much, but the truth is, the weather and avalanches on Everest are so unpredictable. You can't buy into the idea that you have a better chance of survival now than ever before. It just isn't true.

I remember being in the family room of my parents' home before Harold and I were married, when all of a sudden, the television screen was white from the snow of Everest and speckled with color as prayer flags blew in the wind.

I stood in the middle of the room staring at the television as the news covered this tragedy. Mom was sitting on the couch behind me, her face registering shock as she sat frozen by what she was hearing. I stood there only a minute before turning my head, saying "I can't watch this," and walking away.

My mom responded with "I really don't think he should go" and began rambling about the dangers and possibilities. I went into my room, trying my best to shut it all out. My mom followed me to my bedroom door.

"Rachel, I'm serious. I think you need to put your foot down."

It's a weird place to be, supporting your soon-to-be husband in pursuing a dream of his that could very well cost him his life. To this day, I question if it was the right decision. Is there even a right decision in a situation like that? If he died, then clearly it was the wrong decision, but if he succeeded, did that make it the right decision?

I have to commend Harold for his resilience and for trusting that God would close doors if he was making the wrong decision. When Jesus called Peter to walk on water, it required fearlessness to do the unimaginable. When Peter started to doubt, he began to sink. Faith is strengthened through the struggles we face when we depend on God and fully trust Him with the outcome.

If I had let myself hear and read everything about all the Everest tragedies, I don't know if it would have been possible for me to continue to support Harold. I'd like to think I was trusting God with the outcome as well, but I think most of all, I was avoiding fully acknowledging the dangers for the sake of my own sanity. I knew this was something Harold was going to do, so focusing on all the horrible things wouldn't help me. It would only make it harder.

I question whether things would have gone the same way if he had brought up the idea of Everest to me after we were already married. Yes, we were engaged when all this began, but we were not yet husband and wife. It changes things significantly when you become one. It may have changed things for him too.

## HAROLD

Would I still have decided to go if we'd already been married when the idea first came up? Wow, that's a great question. The truth is, I don't know. What I do know is that I was acting completely out of self-interest in my barracks room that day when I decided to climb Everest. Rachel was my first serious relationship, and until that point in my life, I had only made decisions that were in my personal best interest, since I had been responsible for only myself.

Everest had nothing to do with what was best for Rachel or our family. In fact, it stood between Rachel, me, and our future family. I put a deadly wedge between us by choice. At the time, I don't think I really understood what it meant to make decisions based on what was best for our family.

I don't think I started thinking in terms of "us" until quite some time after we were married. In our first year of marriage, we argued about me not being considerate of Rachel and not being a team player.

I have always been a great team player in any team or organization I've been a part of, but when it came to our relationship, I struggled to do the same. I think this holds true for a lot of people. We neglect or take for granted those who are closest to us because we are focusing on what's outside our inner circle.

How could I make a decision that put our marriage in jeopardy without even getting Rachel's input? It's human nature to be self-oriented, but being team-oriented in a marriage is something I needed to conscientiously practice.

If I were given the same opportunity today to climb Everest for the first time, I would undoubtedly say no. Every day, I see the beautiful life I get to live with Rachel, and I would not be willing to risk what we have. I didn't see or appreciate that back then, but I do now.

While the information we were getting indicated the mountain would reopen for the 2016 climbing season, there was no guarantee, so we were operating on faith that we'd even get a chance to try. It was an exciting time because if we did get the go-ahead, the USX team would be among the first teams to climb once the government reopened the mountain.

## RACHEL

Beyond the excitement and adventure was the reality that we had not even been married for a full year, so even though I was supporting him, cheering him on, and helping him in every way I could, did I really want him to go? Definitely not! All my worries of losing him and of possibly being pregnant were intensifying. It was hard to talk with many people about what I was going through because they couldn't relate. I already had so many people telling me, "Wow. I can't believe you're letting him do it. I'd definitely say no." Since my friends and family couldn't understand what I was going through, sharing my deep struggles didn't make a whole lot of sense to me.

All this was swirling around inside my heart and mind as we began the process of saying goodbye—or actually, "See you later, hopefully." I was dreading that moment at the airport when I'd have to let him go. I was praying that my husband would come home safely and that whatever would happen regarding getting pregnant would be in God's perfect timing. But to be honest, that was the easy prayer. I wasn't blindly thinking that if I prayed for Harold to come home safely, I had a guarantee that he would. That wasn't good enough in my eyes because bad things happen. I needed to let go of my own life and put it in God's hands, which is funny because you would think I was praying mostly for Harold's life. In reality, I was praying for my own. I was praying that whatever happened on that mountain, in the end it would all be for God's glory.

Those last couple of weeks before he left had been so hectic that we'd hardly slept at all. You'd think we would have spent those last days together on a little getaway where we could relax and enjoy each other, but the closer his departure date got, the busier we were.

Harold had interviews with CNN, HLN, the Weather Channel, American Sports Network, and Fox. On media days, our mornings would start around 2:30 a.m. If we were lucky, we would get an hour or two of sleep.

The dirty truth of achieving big dreams is that it requires all of you. Often, people see only the victory at the end. What they don't see is all the hard work, risks, late nights, struggles, failures, persistence, doubts, discipline, courage, criticism, disappointments, adversity, tears, rejections, sacrifices, and changes along the way. Next time you find yourself comparing someone else's victory with where you are, remember it was a long road for that person and you may be just starting yours. It's the road to get there that leads to growth and makes the victory worth celebrating.

## HAROLD

On my last day before leaving for Everest, we made our way to my grandmother's house a few hours north of Fort Benning to get together with my family one last time. It unofficially allowed everyone to say goodbye and "I love you" in case things went south on the mountain. Sort of morbid, but true. While eating dinner, I received an alarming voice mail after missing the call and texts from my company commander.

"Your leave request for Everest has not been approved. You need to come back to base *now*."

As it turned out, there was a change in leadership in the chain of command above me and the incoming colonel had to sign off on my trip, so I wasn't officially on leave yet, even though I had signed out of my unit.

A few days earlier, I had received an official memo from my company commander stating that while he was recommending approval for my request, he wasn't supportive of it because "climbing Mount Everest is extremely high risk." He also stated his concern about my sixty-three-day leave, the risk of injury that could affect my training, and the possibility that the rigors of the expedition could leave me unable to qualify for Army Ranger School, which I was scheduled to start soon after I returned. In the end, he still checked *approve* on my leave form.

Due to this change in command way up the ranks, I was told I needed to come back in immediately, so forty-five minutes into our precious time with family, we abruptly had to leave. Goodbyes and "I love yous" were quick as we rushed out the door and drove two hours back to Fort Benning.

It was 9:52 p.m. when we got word that the trip was finally approved. It was literally the final hours before I would get on my flight and head to China.

May 10, 2016

We are two-thirds up the North Col with sheer drop-offs all around us. Even though we're surrounded by ice, ironically, it's hot most of the way up the jagged wall with the sun reflecting off the ice in all directions. The heat is intense and unexpected. I have shed most of my jackets and unzipped my last one so that my bare skin shows. However, in a matter of seven minutes, the weather changes dramatically. A snowstorm blows in, and I scramble to put on all my jackets while gripping the rope that we are still clipped into. There is a sixty-degree temperature change in just moments, with snow blowing in every direction.

We pass a group of Canadian climbers making their descent, a father-son duo among them. Several are struggling. As we carefully unclip carabiners off the ropes, allowing them to pass, we stop and chat a bit with the father, who is trailing at the back of the group. He is a really nice guy with a thick Canadian accent. We share a laugh about how he is looking forward to being back in his warm sleeping bag. Then we press on and soon make it to the top of the ice wall to Camp One. We work our way back to Base Camp, as our acclimatization climb is complete.

The next morning at Base Camp, I wake up to the sound of a Sherpa from another camp yelling for Dave. Word has gotten around that Dave is a doctor and that he regularly helps other international teams diagnose and treat illnesses. This time, the situation seems different. There is an urgency and panic in the Sherpa's voice. The nice Canadian man we passed yesterday is lying motionless in his tent, his son kneeling next to him. Dave pronounces him dead.

Charles MacAdams, sixty-two years old, died of cardiac exhaustion. Charles was a notable Canadian doctor and leaves a family including grandkids behind.* The surrounding mountains serve as an echo chamber for the son's cries, which are heard throughout camp, cutting through the morning's quiet, crisp air.

The rest of the day is solemn and silent. The cries still ring in our ears. Death is in the air. The widow maker has claimed another. This time I feel its grip closing in a little tighter, another reminder of how fast life can change. So much of my experience on Everest will teach me why it's so important to be thankful for the good in life and to not take for granted what I have, especially the people, because time is unrenewable.

I don't share this story with Rachel.

---

* Emma McIntosh, "Calgary Doctor Dies at Everest Base Camp," *Calgary Herald*, June 3, 2016, https://calgaryherald.com/news/local-news/calgarian-doctor-dies-at-everest-base-camp.

# Promises I Can't Keep

**HAROLD**

We got to the airport early in the morning to depart for Nepal. The day was finally upon us. It was time to say goodbye to my love and embark on the daunting endeavor in front of me.

Rachel and I had spent the weekend running in every direction with last-minute errands, staying up late to pack, and jumping through Army bureaucratic hoops. We'd spent hardly any quality time together. The car ride was quiet, mostly because we were completely exhausted. I was excited, and she acted excited for me, though I could see straight through that she was hurting on the inside. She was being strong for me and tough because the moment required her to be. Rachel's courage and strength of character shined throughout this lengthy experience.

We stood in line and hugged and kissed for a while. I told her I loved her and just stared into her eyes, with no idea if these were going to be the last fleeting moments I had on earth with my wife. Right before we said goodbye, she gave me "Open when" letters she'd been working on:

Open when . . .

- You get on the plane
- You're cold
- You get altitude sickness
- You're halfway through the expedition
- You have an awesome day
- You need to pray
- You need a pep talk
- You're thinking about me
- You can't sleep
- You need reassurance
- You need motivation
- You need to know how I'm doing
- You're stressed out
- You need some love
- You need to relax
- You really miss me
- You summit
- You for some reason don't summit

They were her way of being there for me every step of the way. Even if she couldn't physically be there, at least her words could speak some encouragement over me or make me laugh.

I told her to keep busy and not to worry about me, and I promised that I'd be back soon. Although I knew that was a promise I couldn't guarantee.

### RACHEL

I wanted to say "Don't make promises you can't keep," but I didn't want Harold to leave on a sour note. He was right; I was being strong because I had to. I didn't want to break down in front of him and let him walk away knowing he was leaving me when I wasn't okay, so instead, I did my best to show that I was fine. I was probably subconsciously putting up walls, not letting my mind fully accept the weight of this goodbye.

When it was time for Harold and Tommy to board the plane, I was filming a little one-minute video for the team's social media. I was so focused on getting the clips I needed and working up until the last minute that it barely registered that Harold was leaving until he walked toward the security line. Then he was gone.

When I got home, my head hit my pillow and I was out for three hours. As soon as I woke up, I started to work. I'd told Harold on the ride to the airport that he was chasing his dreams, so this was also my time to chase my dreams. For me, that meant putting more time and effort into my YouTube channel. I've always put family first, and in this season, I needed to be by Harold's side, so my vlogs hadn't been as consistent as I wanted. With Harold now gone, it was a great time to pour my time and energy into my work.

I had learned a lot since I posted my first video online. It wasn't until I saw a YouTuber named Bethany Mota on *Dancing with the Stars* that I realized YouTube could actually be a career and a way to make a living. My fun little videos could become more than just a hobby, though I knew it would take time and lots of hard work.

At first, I didn't make any money. But once I shifted into a business mind-set and thought about my YouTube videos as an investment, I knew I would eventually bring returns. At some point, the West Point Girlfriend made her first hundred dollars! That small victory was the push I needed to keep going.

The day after Harold left, it was 6:30 p.m. when I realized I hadn't eaten anything all day because I hadn't slowed down. I got a snack and worked two more hours before exhaustion truly set in. I climbed into bed and snuggled the puppies. Having the dogs was really good for me. With my natural nurturing and maternal instincts, they gave me something to care for and distract me while Harold was away.

A few days later, my friend Morgan came to visit. She brought with her a box full of about fifty letters written by my friends and family members, which were meant to encourage me during the hard times. Her letter to me said,

*Rachel,*

*I'm not sure you know how incredibly loved you are. No matter how long it's been, people love being around your contagious, joyful spirit and want to hold on to your friendship forever. I can't imagine how you're feeling with your love and best friend being away, but I know it's comforting knowing how inspiring he is to so many. But really what else is inspiring is how supportive and involved you have been with Harold's dreams, no matter how hard it is. What an incredible example of a wife you are. In this box are letters from various friends and family of yours. When it's hard, pull one out and let us encourage you like you always do for us. You deserve it.*

I cried when I read the letter, then realized this was the first time I'd cried since Harold left. I felt so supported, and it meant the world to me. It reminded me of the importance of community, especially during these difficult times.

## HAROLD

Excitement filled the air as Tommy and I finally stepped foot in Kathmandu, Nepal. Dave was at the airport waiting for us with a taxi (of sorts). We piled in, Dave in the front and Tommy and I crammed in the back seat with all our climbing gear pressed against the windows. We'd be meeting up with the rest of the team at the hotel.

As the car pulled away from the curb, Dave turned around in his seat. "I have some bad news."

He paused, then said, "The Chinese government has not opened Everest this season, and we don't know when or even if it will be opened at all."

I got a lump in my throat. My heart sank.

"Why?" I asked in a frustrated tone.

"Apparently they are still cleaning up the routes from last year's avalanche," he explained.

I immediately turned my energy to war-gaming and tried to figure out a solution. We had come too far to not find a way to the mountain.

*We will climb from the opposite side. The Nepalese side.*

We were a little late on the climbing window there, but we could still make it. The biggest problem was raising the extra money it would cost because it was more expensive.

I reached out to Connor, one of my best friends from West Point. He was earning his master's degree at Oxford and was one smart guy. Connor was all business, great at making connections with the right people and convincing them to believe in his cause. He'd been the perfect cofounder for USX, always bringing fresh ideas and perspectives to the table and always reliable. As the CFO at USX, he was our secret weapon, putting in tons of hours and carrying the brunt of the fundraising efforts. I sent him a message right away:

> We've got a problem. Tibet route of Everest is closed. May need to climb from Nepalese side. Need to work on a solution.

Connor messaged back:

> I got you; we will find a way.

I love that we both come from the military, because there is a saying that is ingrained in us as young officers: "Find a way or make one." And that's just what he did.

We immediately started reaching out to sponsors to see if we could secure the extra $15,000 to $20,000 it would take for our team to take an alternate route if the Chinese decided not to let us climb. We contacted companies like GovX, a huge e-commerce site for service members, that had been dedicated to helping our cause from day one. That night, I forgot to call Rachel to let her know I had landed in Nepal. I fell asleep slumped over in my hotel chair with a computer and satellite phone in my lap. Everest was kicking my tail, and I hadn't even made it to the mountain yet.

The trip was not starting off smoothly, and to make matters worse, I found out my ascender had been recalled. An ascender is arguably the most important piece of climbing gear and one that you trust more than anything. It's a handheld device connected to your harness that you clip onto the rope and slide (ascend) up before it automatically locks. In the event you fall, it will keep you locked onto the rope so you won't plummet. Word of the recall traveled fast among the climbers in Nepal. It was a specific ascender, and only a small set of serial numbers were affected: 4356 to 6015.

*It's definitely not one of mine.*

I wasn't going to check, but Tommy reminded me that it's better to be safe than sorry. I dug up my ascender buried at the bottom of all my gear. The number was etched in small print: 5,181.

*Oh shoot.*

I am always an optimist, but sometimes it serves as my Achilles' heel. It's my biggest strength but also my biggest weakness. I let my optimism blind me to my present reality. It can distort the decisions I make because I have this "it won't happen to me" mentality. I bend the facts to fit the positive outcome I believe in. I neglect the present because I am overconfident in the future. Overconfidence is a risky trait when you are climbing one of the world's deadliest mountains. Actually, it doesn't matter how deadly your environment; it's never a good mind-set to have.

After I saw the number on my ascender, I panicked. I immediately went into the streets of Nepal and walked from shop to shop trying to find a replacement. It took me two hours, but I found a shop that sold one. The salesman knew I desperately needed one and completely ripped me off. But $160 later, my problem was solved. I glossed over the high price of the equipment when I talked to Rachel later.

Then it happened. We got news that the Tibetan side of Mount Everest was officially opening! I called Rachel to tell her the exciting news. It was go time!

The bad news seemed to be turning around on all sides as we prepared to embark on our ten-day excursion through the Tibetan plateau to reach Everest Base Camp. It was during all this that I heard a story that brought me to tears.

Back in the States, CSM Burnett had an interview with Fox News on behalf of USX, talking about what we were doing and our mission behind it. Immediately following, our publicist, Amy, got a call from a retired service member. He was distressed and having a tough time forming his words. Over and over he kept saying, "I need to talk to that man. I need to talk to that man," referring to CSM Burnett.

Amy put him in touch with Sergeant Major, and it turned out the gentleman had been planning to take his life that day. When he saw CSM Burnett on air talking about our cause, helping Soldiers with PTSD and preventing Soldier suicide, the man felt compelled to reach out. CSM was able to get him connected with some people in his area, and they provided the support he needed. He wasn't the only one who would reach out either.

I was speechless when Amy told me all this. I remember thanking her, hanging up the phone, and looking out my hotel room with a blank stare. Tears started streaming down my face. Our cause had just saved a veteran's life. CSM Burnett had always said that "if we can just save one," it would be worth it. Even to this day, if you ask me what the highlight of my trip was, I will say it was that moment. Our mission was a success before we even made it to the mountain! That experience put everything into perspective.

For a cadet who'd never been affected by PTSD, I could now see how our collective team effort was helping others a world away. The feelings were indescribable. CSM Burnett, a war hero who'd had his own struggles with PTSD and suicidal thoughts, was now actively helping those with the very condition he'd struggled with. God knew this all along. God had intertwined my selfish pursuits with CSM Burnett's triumphs and tribulations and used them together to influence others for His glory.

God brings people into our lives for a purpose. No matter how much of a dreamer we might be, God is crafting our stories into something more beautiful than we could ever write on our own. And while we may not see it now, God does. The only question is, Whom do we want to get the credit for it?

It took me a while after the climb to really acknowledge and praise God as the author of the work He had done in and through me.

### RACHEL

I knew who Harold was when I married him. I knew life with him would be an adventure like none I'd ever been on. From the beginning, he told me he couldn't promise it would always be easy, but it would be worth it. He was right; life together has had its challenges.

Being home without Harold was difficult; the waiting periods were trying, no matter their length. I tried not to dwell on my emotions because I knew this was going to be a pattern in our lives and I needed to figure out a way to not crash and burn each time he left. If we made it through Everest, it wasn't the end of him being gone. He was scheduled to go to Ranger School just a few weeks after he returned, and then life in the Army would have him constantly leaving.

When I find myself dwelling on situations I cannot control, which is often accompanied by negative thoughts, I stop and think of five things I'm thankful for. It's a simple practice, but it always helps change my attitude and turns my day around.

I kept a note card in my Bible with a quote from Brennan Man-

ning that said, "In essence, there is only one thing God asks of us—
that we be men and women of prayer, people who live close to God,
people for whom God is everything and for whom God is enough.
That is the root of peace. We have that peace when the gracious
God is all we seek. When we start seeking something besides Him,
we lose it."*

It was the reminder I needed; all I wanted was to be a woman of
prayer seeking God first. I never liked the saying that God will never give a person more than he can handle, because I knew I couldn't
handle Harold climbing Mount Everest. I wasn't strong enough on
my own, but I knew that God was. If I could get my strength from
Him, I could get through it. It had to be me and God, not me alone.

During one of my more vulnerable moments, when I was really missing Harold, I decided to pull out my box of letters and
read a few. The very first line of one of them read, "The covering
and protection of God is surrounding you right at this moment." I
burst into tears. My eyes became all puffy and my face red as I read
it aloud in front of my camera. The timing of it was powerful, reminding me that in every moment, God is there. No one was with
me in the room, but I could feel the love, support, and encouragement from my friends and family who were thinking about me and
praying for me.

At 2:30 a.m., I got a text from Harold saying he had made it to
Everest Base Camp. I read it with a big smile on my face, feeling his
excitement through the phone. I knew it had to be a pretty awesome
moment for him after all the hard work he had put in, and I was so
happy for him. I just wished I could have been there to celebrate
with him.

This also meant it was officially game time. No more casual
travels; his real journey was about to begin!

---

* Brennan Manning, *The Ragamuffin Gospel* (Colorado Springs, CO: Multnomah,
1990), 46.

**May 11, 2016**

Dave's pulmonary edema and Charles's death remind us all that there is no guarantee of success on this expedition and that the stakes are deadly high. Despite how extensively we've all prepared for this climb, none of us, not even a seasoned climber, is exempt from what Everest might throw at us.

I long to be closer to Rachel. I know she's an incredibly strong woman with an unshakable faith in the Lord—a seasoned climber, if you will—but I ask myself what I've done to prepare her for Everest.

Nothing.

The reality stings. I've leaned too much on the notion that she is strong and will be okay instead of putting in the same effort to help her be successful during this time. Just because she is strong doesn't mean she is invincible.

I could have easily scheduled emails with devotionals and encouraging messages to send to Rachel while I was away, or I could have written her letters like she wrote for me. I should have done better, but I was too focused on Everest, on myself. I put in a tremendous amount of time prepping for what we were about to face on the mountain instead of thinking about what Rachel was about to go through and the strain my climb would put on our marriage and her faith.

I never even asked her what her plans were while I was away, and I certainly didn't help her come up with any. Instead, I left her to do it alone. Preparing relationships for harder times is about transparency, empathy, and intentionality, and I brought none of those to the table.

When we first started dating, Rachel would tell me daily how much she missed me, but I intentionally would never tell her that I missed her. I wanted to be strong for her, but in reality, it was disheartening to her. It took her calling me out on it one day for me to realize that simply saying "I miss you too" showed empathy by acknowledging what we were both feeling. I was recognizing that it's okay to miss each other. It validated her feelings and showed her that we were going through the same thing emotionally.

I failed to do this with Everest.

I took more of a "suck it up, buttercup" approach. Now I'm regretting this.

# The What-Ifs, the How Comes, and the Why Me's

**RACHEL**

The calendar on the table looked bare and bleak. Large empty boxes stretched on and on until (at last!) Harold's estimated homecoming, some sixty days away. I knew what needed to happen.

*It's time to fill this puppy up.*

The biggest piece of advice I can give you if you are going through any sort of long-distance situation with your loved one is to fill your time with quality, life-enriching distractions. Sure, binge-watching several seasons of a television show can distract you for a little bit, and Harold can attest that I can be a binge-watching machine! But these sorts of time fillers aren't going to make you feel good about yourself. You may be alone, but you don't have to feel lonely. Take time to do more with your friends and family and to discover new hobbies that bring you joy.

Over the years, whenever I've been away from Harold, I've learned I cope best when I spend time doing activities that make me a better person. I had to be real with myself. I knew if I chose to stay at home while Harold was climbing Everest, I'd be more aware of his absence as I attempted to go on living our everyday routine.

And I was aware that could lead to resentment. I would feel stuck in a place I didn't want to be. Our house was our home because it belonged to us. If you removed the "us" part, it was just a one-hundred-year-old building in a town far from family. I'd be angry I had been left behind and was missing out on an adventure.

Being a military spouse, you sacrifice so much, from sleep, sometimes purpose, and even career paths. It's easy to feel like you lose a little bit of your own identity as you take on this other identity to follow your husband around for his career, instead of your own.

With each new accomplishment Harold achieved (graduating from West Point, starting USX, and preparing to climb Everest), I started to feel lesser, like I wasn't measuring up in the world's eyes and maybe even my own. Somehow, I was becoming just a wife.

I've always believed in making the most out of every situation and finding the good in it. There's always a positive way to see things, but it must be a choice. You can easily miss out on the good life has to offer if you're always focusing on the bad: the what-ifs, the how comes, or the why me's. Focusing on the difficult things only magnifies the negativity in your life. I find that when you look at your situation with a mind-set of gratitude, your perspective will change.

I was painfully aware of what staying at home might do to me, and I didn't want that. I wanted more for myself. I wanted my own story and my own adventure. I needed a change of pace if I was going to keep my sanity. It's one thing to miss your person and look forward to when you'll be together again, but it's something else to stop living a full life in the meantime. Plus, making the most of the time apart makes the days go by much faster!

I began to think of how I could fill up my calendar. One of the other Army wives who had lived in our neighborhood had just moved out West and said I could visit whenever I wanted. We hadn't been friends long, but I pushed myself outside my comfort zone and texted her to see if her offer still stood. She didn't hesitate and told me to come for a visit!

That's the awesome thing about the military community: everyone understands the ups and downs and the sacrifices required to live this kind of life. We're all eager to support one another, knowing we can't get through it alone.

I wrote "Colorado" across several of the empty calendar boxes. It was a good start, but I still had plenty of days to fill. I knew I wanted to leave the country, so I started googling flights to literally anywhere. I was mostly concerned about the price. It had to be cheap.

Ireland and Iceland were two places I had always wanted to visit. It was a dream of mine to see the northern lights, but I realized I would be pretty bummed if I saw them without Harold. So I decided to save Iceland for another time. I ended up finding a cheap ticket to Ireland.

Harold and I had traveled to nineteen countries together, and I had been to three others with friends and family. I had never set off on my own. I had always been a very independent person, but once I met Harold, I naturally became less independent because it was more fun to do everything with him. Now I was excited for the opportunity to travel on my own. It would stretch me as an independent woman, just like I knew Everest would encourage growth in Harold.

After adding "Ireland" in green ink, my calendar was starting to fill, but I didn't like the few empty squares left, so I texted my three best friends.

Who's down for a girls' trip? I miss you guys!

Everyone was in. We decided on meeting in Nashville, Tennessee, since that was the coolest town of the four places we lived. This also meant we had a free place to stay.

My last stop would be Guatemala. I had gone to Guatemala on my first mission trip five years earlier. What I found there was undeniable joy that shined through the language barrier as the children laughed and played together. I witnessed family after family support and care for one another on a level I had never seen before. Older siblings took care of younger siblings. I saw a girl actually carrying one sibling on her back while holding another's hand as they walked home. I aspired to have a family of my own one day who loved and supported one another to the same degree. A friend asked me to join her, and I was over the moon excited to go back and visit the people who had changed my life years ago.

After much coordinating, I looked at my calendar and felt proud. Not only did I have a lot of distractions to keep me busy, but they all offered new experiences. My own adventures lay ahead. I no longer felt like I was missing out. This was my time to thrive. While my YouTube channel hadn't exactly taken off just yet, I was excited to vlog my entire journey so that when Harold came home, I could show him what I'd been up to.

The day approaches for the beginning of our summit push. We've been on Everest for nearly three weeks now, and I'm trying not to get too caught up in the preclimb jitters. Sleep will be more difficult if I think about the summit. I need to block it out of my mind, focusing on one step at a time.

I'm able to get ahold of Rachel.

"We're trying to summit either May 22 or 23," I tell her. "It all depends on the weather." Since the weather is really unpredictable, I can't give her an exact date.

"Have you read any of the 'Open when' letters I sent?" she asks.

I smile. "I've already read all of them. Except for the summit letter. I couldn't help it. I read one and started missing you, so I just kept reading them. I loved all the funny memories." They'd provided an escape, transporting me for just a moment back into her company.

One of her letters talked about one of the many times we locked our keys in our 2005 gold Toyota Corolla. We were stranded outside, waiting for the locksmith to come. Rachel, being the cute weirdo she is, picked up a stick and pine cone, and we started playing baseball. We giggled and flirted as she hit the pine cone and ran to all the surrounding pine trees that served as bases. I chased her and picked her up from behind as she giggled and screamed.

Little moments like these are some of our favorite memories. Even when life is hard, we always find a way to make it memorable and fun.

This brief memory is a nice diversion for the moment. I can't help thinking about the close call with Dave getting sick and how so much of this climb is out of my hands. I realize more and more that I need God because I am facing a giant I can't handle on my own.

While standing on the side of Everest, I want to ensure I have God by my side. But am I doing the very thing my old baseball coach used to warn our team about when he said, "Never reach out to someone just when you need something from them"?

Is this how I've been living my daily life with God?

I realize it's unfortunately true, but I pray God hears me anyway.

# Beautiful Things Along the Way

**RACHEL**

When I boarded the plane, feeling eager for my solo trip to Ireland, an entire month had passed and Harold's expedition was now halfway through. I'd already experienced a wide range of emotions, but the night Harold called and told me about the snowstorm was the moment when reality truly hit me, when I realized my husband might die.

Harold had told me he was climbing down the mountain to wait out the storm. I noticed he sounded tired, yet he assured me he would be fine. Shortly after this, I received an email from Tommy alerting me to potential dangers. I hadn't been scared until reading that note and learning that Tommy assumed Harold and his team were currently snowed in at Advanced Base Camp. Thankfully, I eventually heard that everything was fine, but the fear had paralyzed me momentarily.

My solo trip to Ireland was my opportunity to see what I was capable of without Harold. I met up with my friend Kate in Belfast. After exploring Northern Ireland and Giant's Causeway, we decided to book a last-minute flight to Scotland, making a one-day trip the very next day. In Scotland, we went for a hike around Arthur's Seat near Edinburgh. Hiking made me feel closer to Harold. We just happened to be taking in two completely different views! That night I pulled out my journal and read what I had written a couple of days before leaving on this trip.

> *Hi, God.*
>
> *I'm struggling and have a thousand thoughts running through my head. I really wish You and I could chat. I miss Harold. To be honest, I feel like I've been handling this whole Everest thing pretty well, much better than I thought I would at least. But then there are times like today when I'm just over it, when I start to feel less of myself because it is so apparent that half of me is away. I hate feeling like this. I'm trying my hardest to stay positive and to live my own adventure, embracing this as an opportunity for growth, yet sometimes it just gets the best of me.*
>
> *Maybe I should look at this as our quality time together, God, instead of looking at it as time without Harold. So, let's make this time about us! Lord, teach me Your ways. I love You, and I put You first! When I am stubborn, remind me of this, that being close to You is all I really want and it takes time and effort, but it's always worth it.*

I needed that reminder. In the lonely moments, I was focusing on the empty feeling of Harold's not being by my side instead of the fullness of God's presence with me each step of every day. I knew it was okay for me to admit I was feeling sad, but I didn't want to let those negative feelings drown me. Choosing to learn and grow from an experience doesn't mean you have to deny the very real feelings that come from enduring your time of trial. I felt what I needed to feel and then chose to refocus. Changing the direction of my thoughts helped me feel more in control of my situation.

On my last day in Ireland, I took a hike along a narrow trail, overlooking the seaside cliffs on the outskirts of the small town of Howth. I stopped to take in the view, sitting at the edge of the cliff with my feet dangling over the side. The waves crashed against the rocks below and then trickled down like mini waterfalls. I unzipped the top of my backpack and pulled out my journal to write.

*I'm glad I can just sit here and take a moment to breathe and reflect. I'm really proud of myself for having the guts to just go off on my own. I think one of my fears is going through life alone, which sounds weird since I am blessed beyond measure in my marriage with Harold. Life is so exciting, and I have no idea where it will take me; kinda like this trip. I had never even heard of Howth until I got here, and here I am taking in one of the best views. I think You do that with our lives, God. Life may not always go the way we planned, but we get to see some beautiful things along the way.*

I stood up and continued my hike, smiling the whole way. It truly was one of the most beautiful and peaceful places I had ever been. I thought how much Harold would have loved it because it was the perfect kind of walk for a daydreamer—easy to get lost in your thoughts and feel inspired. The trail was lined with beautiful yellow flowers, but I learned the hard way those little suckers would sting if you touched them.

I had been walking for a long time and needed to head back, so I took a cut-through path I spotted and hoped for the best. I was praying not to get lost out there alone next to some cliffs before the sun went down and I missed my train back to Dublin.

I spotted a gray stone bench up ahead. As I got closer, I saw it had the words "Find God in All Things" etched across it. I looked up and gave a little smirk to God. It was the perfect way to describe what this Ireland adventure had meant for me.

I was reminded of a verse I lean on during challenging times:

"Consider it pure joy, my brothers and sisters, whenever you face trials of many kinds, because you know that the testing of your faith produces perseverance" (James 1:2–3, NIV). It was a beautiful reminder that no matter what I'm experiencing in life—highs, lows, or in-betweens—God is always with me, and there is something to gain from every experience.

I made my journey home, first to Lakeland, Florida, for a quick visit with my parents, then back to Georgia to recover for a few days before heading off to Nashville and finally to Guatemala! Harold's summit push would be starting soon, but I felt like the burden of worry and fear that I'd been carrying had lifted, at least for now.

Before leaving on our expedition, CPT Matt Hickey and I discussed the realities of one of our team members dying on Everest.

"If the team makes it to the summit with one of the first active-duty Soldiers and one of the first combat-wounded vets ever to get there, that will probably make national news," Matt said. "And that would be an incredible accomplishment, both for USX and for every Soldier we're climbing for."

"But . . . ," I said, seeing where he was going with this.

"But if, God forbid, something bad happens and we lose a combat-wounded Soldier or a novice climber gets into trouble, that will undoubtedly make headline news too. That would be very damaging for USX and even worse for the issue of Soldier-PTSD awareness. If our cause gets associated with some kind of tragic disaster, you can bet that's what the headlines will focus on."

It was a great point and a polite way of saying we have to be super careful on the mountain because attaching yourself to a cause can have negative consequences too.

We will eventually learn that an Australian woman, Dr. Maria Strydom, will die after nearly reaching the summit of Mount Everest. Her cause is to prove that vegans can do anything. An unfortunate backlash from the media will occur and damage the cause she is trying to stand for. It will serve as a valuable lesson to us as we press on in our own awareness mission.*

Knowing the ramifications of our actions is important. Being on the same page and communicating clearly and consistently as a team facing extreme conditions are absolutely critical. The potential consequences of failing to communicate can be disastrous, even deadly.

Most of us can point to bad choices we've made in life, both large and small, that became glaringly clear in hindsight—to the point that we wondered what we were thinking in the first place. This happens to us at the final camp before the summit, Camp Three, when the situation turns dangerous for our team very quickly.

* Travis M. Andrews, "Woman Trying to Prove 'Vegans Can Do Anything' Among Four Dead on Mount Everest," *Washington Post*, May 23, 2016, www.washington-post.com/news/morning-mix/wp/2016/05/23/woman-trying-to-prove-vegans-can-do-anything-among-three-dead-on-everest-two-more-missing-and-thirty-sick-or-frostbitten.

## Summit Fever

**RACHEL**

I was in my car driving to Nashville when my phone rang. I thought it was probably my mom calling. I hadn't heard from Harold all day and didn't think he was going to be able to call, so when I saw it was him, I was really excited. My voice pepped up when I answered the phone. "Hey, hunny!" I said.

I was expecting his usual chipper "Heyyyy!" but as soon as Harold started talking, I could hear the devastation in his voice. He told me he was sick and wouldn't be able to make the summit push. He didn't know if he'd be able to go at all since there was such a tiny window and his body was in no condition to climb. He was crushed.

**HAROLD**

The morning we were leaving for our summit push, the start of our three-day grueling trek to the top, I awoke to my stomach in knots. I barely had enough time to make it out of my tent and pull my pants down before my bowels gave way. It was bad. My stomach was killing me. I had vicious diarrhea.

*I must have a stomach bug,* I thought.

It was a common condition up there, people suddenly struck with diarrhea, vomiting, and weakness. It could be food poisoning, a virus, or bacterial contamination. The cause didn't really matter. I knew that if I were to climb, things could turn deadly, as it would deplete my energy and could cause me to stop for frequent bathroom breaks. What mattered was getting over it. Quickly.

I immediately started taking meds and crushing water as fast as I could, but I was miserable. Nothing helped. I crawled out of the tent but couldn't walk more than a few feet without having to find a rock to stagger behind, peel off the layers, and go to the bathroom. I didn't feel like I could eat anything. I was going to have to make a hard call because I knew I couldn't leave for the summit that day.

I found the team. I had to force the words out. "I can't go."

They looked at me, eyes wide, but they could tell by my face what was going on. It's hard to hide that special kind of misery.

"You guys feel free to go ahead. If the weather allows, I can leave with my Sherpa in a day or two when I feel better, but I don't want to hold you up."

"Wait, let's look at the weather first," one of them said. "If we can find another weather window that works, then we want to go as a team." The others nodded. Out of the entire season, climbers typically have only a few days of good conditions to climb to the summit. The backward clock had already started.

It was killing me, but I knew I couldn't climb in my current condition. Besides feeling weak and not being able to eat, there was no way I could climb while so violently ill. Staring up at the highest point on Earth, my spirits were at the lowest in my life. I called Rachel.

I am pretty sure that for the first minute of the call, I couldn't even get any words out. I was just sobbing. I sat in my tent with my hands over my face, the phone on speaker in my lap. I could see the summit, but I wasn't going to be able to go. I needed Rachel to help me through this.

**RACHEL**

I had a lot of thoughts running through my head. First, I felt absolutely horrible for him. To work so hard for years, just to be defeated by a stupid stomach bug. It felt like a sad, pathetic joke. Of course, I didn't think it was a joke, and I'm sure no one else did either, but I knew Harold was probably feeling like it was.

He'd been healthy the entire trip up until now. I tried my best to comfort him, praying for him over the phone and assuring him that he was still making a big impact even if he didn't summit. The fact that the team had raised all this awareness for PTSD and Soldier suicide was invaluable. He was still feeling down, so I understood that he didn't want to talk for very long. My heart felt heavy as we hung up the phone because I knew he was hurting and there wasn't anything I could do about it.

Then I thought maybe this was God's way of protecting Harold, and if that was the case, I was thankful. Having my husband come home safely was a big win in my book. I knew Harold would probably never see it that way, which then turned my mind to a new thought.

*If he isn't able to summit, he'll want to go back next year.*

That was not an option for me. I wouldn't put myself through all this again. I'd have to tell him no, which I didn't want to do. But at least in the present moment, I didn't have to worry about the dangers of him climbing, because he couldn't.

The next day, my friends and I were exploring Nashville and had plans to go to a Carrie Underwood concert at the Grand Ole Opry that evening. I had been waiting all day for an update from Harold, hoping his spirits would be up a little, but I figured I wouldn't hear anything until evening, as that was the normal time he called. And wouldn't you know it, as soon as Carrie Underwood walked on stage, my phone started vibrating. It was Harold.

I ran out of the concert and picked up the phone as fast as I could. He greeted me with a "Heyyy, hunny!" His happy, chipper voice was back, and I was very confused.

"Well, don't you sound happy," I said, thinking he had just turned his attitude around, which was nice but also a bit surprising. I thought he'd still need some comforting.

"I feel so much better!" he said with unbelievable enthusiasm. "We're leaving in ten minutes for the summit push."

*What?*

I immediately started crying. None of this made any sense. Even though he sounded energetic and like himself again, it completely threw me off. "I don't understand. You were just sick," I said through my tears.

He said something as he tried to convince me his body was magically better and he was capable of climbing, but it all blurred together. My mind couldn't process what was going on. I didn't see how his body could possibly be healthy enough to climb. Sure, I was glad he was feeling better, but I questioned if he was telling me the truth. How could he be ready for the summit push?

"You promise you're okay to climb?" I asked repeatedly, the distress clear in my voice.

Harold assured me, "I'm feeling 100 percent better. I'm feeling strong!"

The cheer and enthusiasm never left his voice as he promised that he was telling the truth, that he was healed. I was worried he may have caught something much worse than a stomach bug: summit fever.

The team was about to leave, so he had to go. This would be the last time I would hear from him until he got back down the mountain. *If he got back.* It could easily be our last goodbye. Still sobbing, I told him I loved him at least three more times before he finally hung up.

I stood there feeling numb and helpless, still questioning what he'd just told me. In my heart, I had to believe that he wouldn't do something stupid, that he wouldn't try to summit unless he really was feeling strong enough to do it. Surely he wouldn't risk what he cared about most, his family. I tried hard to focus on that.

I called both his parents to give them the news. I didn't want to freak out his mom, so I composed myself before telling her the "good news" that he was healthy and getting ready to summit. When I spoke to his dad, I was a little more candid about what was going on. He assured me that if Harold said he was healthy and okay to climb, he was.

From that point on, I was more nervous than ever about the summit push. I went back to the concert and sat there with a blank stare as "Mama's Song" played.

*He makes promises he keeps*
*No he's never gonna leave*

Tears streamed down my face as I did my best not to break out in an audible sob. Luckily, the lights were dim and I could wipe away my tears without my friends noticing. I still had a few more songs to pull myself together. I didn't have the emotional energy just yet to share what I was going through.

## HAROLD

I woke up that day feeling significantly better after rehydrating, taking medicine, and getting plenty of rest. I knew the team was leaving that morning, and I thought I could still make the summit.

When I spoke to Rachel, I could hear the fear in her voice. She questioned my health and my honesty. And she was right: I was lying. Even though I wasn't completely over the stomach bug and still felt a little weak, there was no way I was going to throw away my dream and all my work and sacrifice from the past two years. I had to lie to myself and to Rachel about my health to try to selfishly accomplish my dream, all while limiting the worrying of my loved ones. This moment—deciding to attempt the summit without my full health or strength—was by far the most anxious I had been the entire trip. I was excited and terrified.

In reality, I had come down with something even more dangerous than a stomach bug. Rachel was right; I had summit fever. A desperate case of it. Summit fever is when a climber has such an intense desire to make it to the top that he is no longer able to make reasonable decisions and ignores clear indications that he should stop his pursuit to the summit.

If required, I would have done anything to get to the summit of Mount Everest, sacrificing my marriage and future. I was numb to logic. Numb to love. The only thought in my mind was *I have to get to the top. It is now or never.* I had lost myself and my concept of what was truly important in my unwavering pursuit of my Everest dream. It was the deadliest of sicknesses to have on Everest, with bodies lining the path to prove it.

I thought about the conversation I had with Tommy the day before as we contemplated the possibility of my death. He told me he had stayed up three hours the previous night thinking about my eulogy. We joked about freezing my sperm up on Everest or having our dog Ranger tell Rachel the news, but the truth was, that conversation was necessary.

"I have to leave a message for Rachel before I go," I said. "I'm going to do it on my audio recorder so she can hear my voice."

Tommy nodded.

We decided Tommy couldn't deliver that kind of news over the phone. He would travel to our home and arrange to have Rachel's mom and dad sitting beside her.

After that conversation, I waited a few minutes and then headed out of the tent to find a quiet place on the edge of camp. I sat perched on a rock with the sun reflecting off Everest toward me. I pulled out the audio recorder and started my goodbye message to Rachel.

"Hey, hunny. I wanted to leave you a little voice note. We're hoping to leave tomorrow to go up Everest, and I just wanted to leave you this in case something not so good happens to me up there and I have a tough time getting down. I guess if you're listening to this, it's because I'm dead. And I really just wanted to tell you that I love you so much. I love you SO much! I've got tears coming down my face right now.

"You know, I can't say I know why this happened, but I still believe in a big God and He did it for a reason. He does everything for a reason. I can promise you at this moment I'm doing all right. I'm probably walking on some pretty golden streets and looking down at you. I'm sure you're probably bawling your eyes out, but just know that I'm looking down at you from above. I'm sure I'm sitting next to God and telling Him to try to help your YouTube channel get big so you can make a big impact.

"I love you so much, and honestly, I'm so thankful for the past year with you. It's been the greatest time of my entire life. I mean, just getting to spend it with you has been unbelievable. You've taught me so much; I've learned so much from you, and I'm so grateful. I guarantee you in those final breaths, however I died, I was thinking of you and our time together. I probably died with a smile on my face, thinking about you and all of our funny and crazy memories . . . .

"Don't be mad at God or mad at yourself for letting me

go. This is something that I felt called to do. God definitely had me here for a reason. Don't think for a second it wasn't worth it. I was following my dreams of trying to make an impact on other people. Don't blame anyone for that. I'm so blessed, the life I've had. The life I've lived up to this point, it's been amazing. God let me be a part of your life, which has been a highlight. . . . I love you, and I'm not sure if I should end this because you're probably like 'Please don't let the recording end.' Just please, please, please know that you can make a big impact and continue to follow your dreams. I love you so much, and I'll see you again one day. I'll see you again. . . . I love you. Don't miss me too much.

"Dear God, please take care of my wife."*

It was really difficult to get the words out. How do you send a final message to the love of your life? My eyes were red as tears rolled down my face. So many emotions tore through me. My heart ached. I hurt deeply for Rachel and for what I know she will have to go through if I die, but in the message, I wanted to remain strong for her because I know she will lean on it to help her get through the pain.

I recorded my message to Rachel just yesterday, and now the moment is here. I give Tommy a hug, go to the bathroom one last time, get on my gear, and leave with our team for our summit push.

God, this is it. Please help me.

* Watch the actual goodbye recording at Earls.org/ByeLove.

# The Death Zone

**RACHEL**

Now, as I'm writing this book three years later, is the first time I've listened to that message. I knew Harold left a message for me, but I could never bring myself to listen to it. Everything was still so fresh, and it's easy to get sucked back in time and feel like I'm living those moments again. The fear of losing my husband is a feeling I don't want to revisit.

When he said the part about not being mad at myself, I instantly started to cry. I would have been. I would have been so angry at myself, and I would have gone back over everything in my head, questioning what I hadn't seen clearly. I would have needed to hear what he said, but I'm so thankful I didn't listen to that message until now.

For the record, let me just say that if he had died, I don't at all believe it would have been because God did it, nor do I think that's what Harold meant. When terrible things happen, I believe we can see God bringing good out of them if we are open and willing, but I don't believe He chooses for those bad things to happen.

## HAROLD

After the emotional goodbye phone call with Rachel, our team began our trek up the North Col yet again. This time, it was not an acclimatization climb; it was the real deal. The climb was grueling. And the steepness made it unforgiving. We staggered into Camp One in our climbing buddy teams and lay down in our tents from utter exhaustion. I didn't even have time to fully open the frozen Snickers bar I had been daydreaming about the whole way up before a Sherpa yelled to us, "Help! A climber is injured!"

Without hesitation, we threw our boots back on and headed toward the action. A British climber on his descent from the summit had been severely injured, was out of oxygen, and was lying in the snow. Chad set up a pulley system with the help of several international climbers to drag the man to Camp One. We later got news that the man made it down and was escorted to a local hospital. Another reminder of the deadly nature of the climb.

The next day, we put our oxygen tanks on our backs and strapped on our fighter pilot oxygen masks as we began our ascent to Camp Two. It was both physically and mentally exhausting as we slogged up a wide and gradual snow slope for six to eight hours to reach camp.

On my way into camp, I came close to collapsing. I thought about the Canadian father who'd collapsed and died. This fear motivated me to gut it out a few more steps. I'd never felt more exhausted in my life. I was surprised I was feeling this depleted; something felt off. Was it because I'd been sick that made climbing this excruciating? I had to sit down on the snow slope and rest before continuing on to my tent that thankfully had been set up earlier by Sherpas. For the first time in my life, I didn't want to move. *Whatever,* I thought. *I'll just sit here.*

As I panted for air, my breathing was so heavy that ice crystals formed on the outside of my fighter pilot mask. In that moment, I understood why some people just sit down on Everest and never get up again.

I forced myself to get up and try again, but I made it only another ten feet before having to sit down and rest again. The amount of utter exhaustion I felt was unexplainable. I was now only five feet away from my tent, but I didn't even have enough energy to get in. I just sat there for a long while and eventually crawled the rest of the way.

It was 8:30 p.m., and all I wanted to do was pass out. As I took the twenty-pound oxygen tank off my back, I realized it had been on the wrong setting! I'd been climbing all day without any oxygen support at more than twenty-four thousand feet. It was a clear mental lapse on my end. I knew that the higher in altitude I climbed, the harder it would be to use cognitive skills. I still had five thousand feet in vertical height to make the summit. Since I still had a full tank, I cranked the Os up high and fell into a blissful and relaxing sleep.

## RACHEL

Two days after the call from Harold saying he was going for the summit push, I was in the airport waiting for my flight to Guatemala. I didn't intentionally plan for my Guatemala trip to fall while Harold was summiting, but that's how it happened.

One of the reasons I was drawn back to that country is because of the resilience, strength, and perseverance the Guatemalan women demonstrate on a daily basis. Back in the '80s, a vicious war broke out and many of the men in the village were brutally murdered. Bullet holes scarred the church walls and ceiling where these villagers worshipped, serving as a constant reminder of all the loved ones who lost their lives. The women were left to carry on and provide for their families, which they did by weaving cloth and making beautiful clothing, bags, and other items to sell in the market. Their faith was not shaken. They continued to attend church, despite what they'd lost, as their faith carried them through these dark times. They are women I aspire to be like, women who appreciate life and family for the gifts they are, who never give up, and who always push forward for the sakes of their families.

The Guatemalan women carry their babies on their backs using cloth they make. One day during my visit, I asked one of the moms to teach me how to do it. She giggled and asked if I was pregnant. I said I didn't think so but that I wanted to have babies soon. She laughed and told me to wait a moment, then walked into her house. She came out with the biggest smile on her face as she held a baby doll out to me. I stepped forward, took that sweet baby doll in my arms, and made my best attempt at slinging it behind my back and wrapping the cloth tightly to hold it in place. It was a silly moment but also a flash of the future I hoped I'd have.

Out in the village, I knew I wouldn't get any cell service and would have only a few opportunities to stop at an internet café to check for updates from Harold. I was still vlogging my whole journey, but I put a hold on uploading the videos until I got home. I left Harold's cousin Kirby in charge of the climb's social media while I was away.

It was the absolute worst timing for me, the media person, to be out of touch, since it was during the two most dangerous parts of the expedition: the summit and the descent. On the other hand, for me personally, as Harold's wife, Guatemala was the best place I could be. I could imagine the constant fearful chatter and questioning happening back home and the way I would have been drawn to fixate on the fears.

While I loved managing social media for USX, by default, friends and family members expressed their worries and concerns to me. I was already dealing with my own worries, so the added burden of everyone else's fears was too much. Being in Guatemala was healthy for me. It allowed me to focus on something outside Everest, to escape in a way.

The timing of this trip felt like a coincidence at the time. When my friend asked if I wanted to tag along, I could feel a nudge from God to go. It was the same feeling I'd had when I felt called to Guatemala the first time. Looking back now, I know it was all part of God's perfect timing.

## HAROLD

As we climbed toward Camp Three, the last camp before the summit, I continually had to stop to use the bathroom, thanks to my lingering stomach virus. An Doja, my Sherpa, had to pull my pants down for me and hold my gear as I squatted next to him. He's seen way more of me than either of us ever expected. Our process was slow going, and my pack felt heavy in my weakened state.

Prior to our summit push, we decided not to take our radios beyond Base Camp. We were told by returning climbing teams that we would have good cell phone service once we reached Camp One. Our thinking was logical but not practical. On a rigorous high-altitude climb, you want your pack to be as light as possible, and leaving the radios saved some weight. With just cell phones, we reasoned, we'd be able to communicate both with one another and with our families when we reached the summit.

What we had forgotten was that we all climbed at different speeds. The practicality of pulling out a cell phone in subzero temperatures and calling the climbing team in front of us was not realistic. Additionally, we discovered that our phones don't work well in extreme elements. To our dismay, most of our phones stopped working just above Camp One. This meant we had no way to communicate.

When An Doja and I arrived at Camp Three, it was late in the evening. We had about four hours before we would begin our final push to the summit. The plan was to climb through the night and summit by sunrise. Our USX team was split between two tents, with our Sherpas in other tents. The wind was howling and whipping the tents, as we were now exposed to the infamous North Face of Everest. It was hard to hear, and it would have been nice to simply press a button on our radios and talk to the tent fifteen feet from us. Instead, we yelled back and forth to confirm a 10:00 p.m. departure time.

By 9:50 p.m., I was geared up and sitting with my feet sticking outside the tent while I strapped on my boots. I was exposing myself to the elements, as putting the big, bulky boots with crampons on inside the tent would have ripped the floor to shreds. All climbers know that once you leave the warmth and safety of your tent, you need to depart as soon as possible to mitigate the risk of exposure to the extreme cold. In the death zone, where the altitude and lack of oxygen take such an excessive toll on the human body, keeping precisely to the schedule is essential, especially when attempting to summit.

To my surprise, I learned Dave and Chad weren't ready to leave, and for good reason. They didn't have enough water, boiled from the snow and then purified, to last them the next twenty-plus hours of climbing to the summit and then getting back down out of the death zone. Their equipment was subpar, and there was a miscommunication with their Sherpa.

*How come we didn't know this sooner?* I wondered. Did one of them shout the update in the wind, and we just didn't hear it?

This was the first ripple created by our deficiency in communication. I've learned the hard way that when you make one mistake in hazardous conditions, there's a very good chance it will be followed by second-order mistakes and possibly several more rounds after that. Over the next seventy-two hours, the ripple effect would continue to spread outward, and several climbers from our team would be in life-threatening predicaments following the initial bad decision.

Please learn from my mistake, and never replace common sense with anything else. First, when you make a decision, you should always be able to check the "because it makes sense" box. If you can't, it's a dumb decision. Not bringing communication equipment did not check that box. It was dumb. Plain and simple. Second, communicating is not just yelling at another person, assuming the message has been understood clearly and entirely. That is talking *at* someone. It gives the perception that communication has taken place, when, in fact, it may not have. Communication requires taking the time to confirm that both sides are in sync with each other.

By the time we figured out why Dave and Chad were delayed, we'd had our feet outside in subzero temperatures for over fifty minutes. Our Sherpas stood outside, waiting to go. To limit further unnecessary exposure time, we decided to break into two teams.

"We've got to depart now," I hollered toward their tent. "We'll link up with you at the vertical steps approaching the summit."

I was referring to several technically difficult points on the mountain that almost always take additional time to navigate. Our first team left by moonlight through the Exit Cracks, a series of gullies and rock ledges leading to the summit ridge. It wasn't that steep, but the ropes and anchors were well worn, and extreme focus was necessary.

It wasn't long before the first mishap. Something snagged my goggles, knocking them off my face and sending them toppling from rock to rock on the cliffs below, straight out of sight into the darkness. A rational person would have turned around right then, knowing that climbing without goggles is crazy. A snowstorm could be detrimental, causing blindness. I didn't let it stop me, however, and made it past the First Step, the first of three technically challenging vertical pitches.

Around this point, we managed to link up as a team. I learned later that my goggles had toppled over a hundred meters in pitch darkness and landed at Dave's feet. I could see their headlamps below but didn't know Dave had picked up my goggles and put them in his pack. He hadn't realized they were mine, and they remained in his pack even when we joined up. Dave was in the back of the climbing formation, and I was in the front, so he couldn't see that I'd lost my goggles. What we didn't realize was that in addition to Dave catching my goggles, he'd also caught a stomach bug.

In complete darkness at twenty-eight thousand feet, with the wind whipping and snow pelting our masked faces, yelling didn't work very well, but we had no other way to communicate. Chad and Dave, now moving at a significantly slower pace, along with their Sherpa, fell behind the rest of the climbing team. We didn't realize just how far behind they were until we were nearing the summit. Dave was in rough shape and not getting any better, but he pressed on. Not knowing what Dave was going through, the climbers in the front kept going, putting him at a greater risk of something going fatally wrong.

The climb gets significantly tougher at the Second Step. It's almost impossible without the sketchy fixed ladder the Chinese put there years ago. The climb up the ladder was challenging, but we'd heard the way down was even more dangerous. It was notorious for the views of the steep drop-offs and the lifeless bodies of fallen climbers clearly visible below.

The voice of my Sherpa jerked me from my determined concentration as we approached the summit pyramid. "I can't find the ropes," he said, referring to the preset ropes anchored to the cliff side.

We needed the ropes to keep us safe on this final stretch to the summit, but fresh snow had covered them. The Sherpas shined their lights back and forth as they probed the snow with ice axes. Several tense moments passed. With nothing to clip into, this could be the end of our expedition.

*If we can't find the ropes, I'm going to try anyway.*

Meeting the other climbers' eyes, I saw them nodding in agreement. We could see the summit now. We would press on with no ropes on a cliff face on top of the world in pitch darkness with a possible 7,500-foot free fall. It was madness. And we made this decision with zero hesitation. Summit fever was burning ferociously now in all of us.

Right before we began to move without the ropes, one of the Sherpas found them and we were able to clip in and continue. Would I have made it without the fixed ropes? I'm not sure. But I was so focused on reaching the summit that I was willing to take a very big risk anyway.

May 24, 2016

Finally, I am here, standing in the exact destination I have dreamed about for two years. No ground on earth stands higher than the ground my feet are standing on: the summit of Mount Everest. The sun has just started to spill over the horizon on the last few steps as I make it to the peak.

Against a backdrop of breathtaking beauty, I pull out of my pocket the dog tags of Major Chris Thomas, one of the Soldiers we are climbing in honor of, who served four combat tours in Iraq and Afghanistan and died in an avalanche in 2015. I place them at the summit beneath the strings of colorful prayer flags. Then I pull out my cell phone to try to call Rachel, but it still won't turn on. So I sit back to take it all in.

After two years in the making, thousands of hours of work, countless sleepless nights, dozens of people telling me I couldn't do it, and pints of sweat shed from training, I am finally here. I stand on the shoulders of many others who believed in me. It is the climax of all my hard work, and although I am at the intersection of my dream and reality, I struggle to fully enjoy the moment. The view is indescribable, with the white Himalayan landscape spread before me as far as I can see, but it feels sort of anticlimactic. Now that I have made it, all I really care about is getting back down and going home to Rachel. Plus, it is really, really cold.

Back when I was a cadet training for Everest, my mom gave me a sign that said, "If you don't climb the mountain, you can't enjoy the view." I thought it was inspiring, and every day I pictured the view of the snow-capped mountains from the summit. Now that I've actually climbed the mountain and can see the view, I realize I've misinterpreted that quote. The view is not the reward. The reward is the person I've become by facing the mountain, the struggles that have shaped me, the adversity that's defined me, the obstacles that have tried to stop me but failed, the naysayers who've knocked me down but been unable to keep me down. Having a dream, finding a way to accomplish it, and knowing the transformation that it's had on me . . . this is my reward.

It will take a while for all this to truly sink in. For now, all I can think about is getting back down safely. The truth stares back at me. Getting down will be harder than getting to the summit. Ninety-five percent of deaths and accidents on Everest occur not in going up the mountain but in coming down.

I take one last look over the mountains, at the curvature of the earth, and I feel the deep ache filling my soul as my heart yearns for Rachel. I want to get off this mountain now, but I have a long way to go.

As I will soon find out, the way down will be the greatest threat to my future with Rachel, and our team will be split up, each of us left to fight for survival.

# Snow Blind

**HAROLD**

I was standing on a ledge not much wider than a snowboard, the rock dropping away to empty space just inches from my feet, as An Doja sat in the snow haphazardly trying to put his mittens on backward.

*What on earth is he doing?*

Before I had time to shout the question out loud, An Doja lifted his head and said something. His words were swallowed by a fierce gust of wind.

"What?" I called out.

"Can't see!" came An Doja's reply as he motioned toward his eyes.

It took a few minutes for my oxygen-hungry brain to process this information. My strong and cool-headed Sherpa guide couldn't see his mittens. Realization dawned slowly, but once it did, the implications were perfectly clear. *An Doja isn't just talking about mittens. He literally can't see at all.*

We had left our tents around 11:00 p.m. the night before to start our bid for the summit, then reached the top of the world at 7:42 a.m. We had now been descending for several hours. I was mentally and physically exhausted and still a very long way from safety. Climbers always talk about how things can get very bad very quickly on the mountain, and that's exactly what was happening right now. The only person who could get me down the mountain just lost his eyesight.

*This is how people die on Everest*, I thought.

As a West Point cadet, I'd been trained to rely on many skills and processes to navigate complex situations, and there was an acronym we followed: METT-T, Mission Enemy Terrain Troops-Time. How would that work here?

What is the Mission? *Get to the bottom of the mountain without dying.*

What is known about the Enemy? *They don't call it the death zone for nothing.*

How will Terrain and weather affect the operation? *Either they'll kill us or they won't.*

What Troops are available? *One Sherpa, current status: blind. Other teammates: location unknown, spread out on the mountain.*

How much Time is available? *Best estimate, less than enough.*

*Well, that isn't exactly helpful.* Things were definitely not looking good. I was scared out of my mind, but thinking about it wasn't going to help me or An Doja. Nor was dwelling on the fact that my Sherpa had been sharing his protective goggles with me ever since the rock face ripped my own pair from my face during our ascent. We traded back and forth between his goggles and sunglasses, ultimately leaving us both with insufficient protection from the elements.

The glare of the sun off the ice in the thin Himalayan atmosphere was searing our retinas, while our eyeballs were under siege from wind-whipping clouds of snow crystals, which burned like liquid fire on the exposed skin on our faces. The dual-forced assault had taken its toll. An Doja had gone snow blind. He had the knowledge but not the sight. I had the will and determination to push on but no way to find my way down.

After pulling his mittens off again, An Doja rubbed his hands together, then pressed them against his eyes.

"An Doja, your hands will freeze!" I called, making my way toward him as I pulled up the slack of the rope anchored in the wall so it would not get caught in my crampons.

I unzipped my yellow-and-blue expedition suit, specifically designed to withstand the treacherous conditions that exist at eight-thousand-meter peaks. Built for extremes, the down-filled suit is like a super-powered onesie with a hood. It had held up great so far, except for some crampon rips at the bottom that I tried my best to patch. I put one hand on An Doja's shoulder and pulled him toward me. The suit shielded him enough to allow him to warm the ice crystals on his eyes.

I pulled the goggles from my head and scraped at them with my fingers. Between the unrelenting drifting of powdery snow and my own exhalations forced upward from my oxygen mask, the goggles were hopelessly iced over. Without them, I ran the risk of becoming snow blind too, but when I put them on, everything from the Himalayan vista spreading out before me to my own black-and-yellow boots transformed into a blur of shapes and shadows. It was easier to see with the sunglasses, but then I was more exposed to the elements. We traded so An Doja could have the goggles to warm his eyes and I could have the sunglasses to see better for a while.

The weather had taken a turn, with clouds rolling in from the north and gale-force winds blasting into us. An Doja and I were still in the oxygen-starved death zone. We had no way to communicate with our team members or with Base Camp. I was far from an experienced mountaineer, but I knew that to remain where we were made our survival impossible. In reality, my body was already beginning to shut down.

At an altitude of over twenty-six thousand feet, the combined forces of oxygen deprivation and changes in atmospheric pressure cause the human body to go into a radical mode of self-decay. Blood flow to the muscles and brain is reduced, throwing the physical body into a state called necrosis. Blood thickens like syrup, cells begin to die, and after some time, organs begin to shut down.

I understood the science of the death zone as well as the next guy, but nothing could have prepared me for the sight of what's been called Rainbow Valley. I had passed through it in pure ignorance on the ascent due to the utter darkness. But early on the way down, I saw what I thought was a blue duffel bag that had been left behind in the snow, just a foot or so from where I was walking. Only as I was passing it did I realize with sickening clarity that the shape was a corpse, its limbs and head buried in snow and ice so that only the back of the torso in a blue down jacket was visible.

As the sun rose higher in the sky, I noticed more bodies below in the distance: spots of color amid the gray rock and white snow. Some of these climbers had slipped and fallen over the edge. Some had become disoriented with altitude sickness and gone the wrong way. Some had dropped from exhaustion.

For hundreds of people, Everest is their final resting place because it is too expensive and risky to move their bodies. The dead range from the poorly prepared to world-class mountaineers. I knew that any one of those splashes of color could be me.

An Doja gave a thumbs-up and a nod. "I'm good to go."

It was time to get moving.

Every step was agony. I tried to block from my thoughts any factor that was not in my personal control.

The vicious gusts of wind that were shoving me off balance and making my bones ache with cold.

*Not in my control.*

The drunken zombie effect caused by the altitude that was sapping my strength and breath and draining the life from my blood.

*Not in my control.*

The burning pain in my toes that was giving way to numbness. *Not in my control.*

The need to keep moving down the mountain at all costs, no matter how agonizing . . . that was something I *could* control. So I focused every ounce of concentration I had on my feet. Everything else fell away as my life narrowed into a single repeated objective: *Take a step. Take another step. Take another step.*

I thought about Rachel, 9,487 miles away and at this very moment likely worried out of her mind about me. I had passed along a request earlier to some Sherpas heading down from Camp Three for Tommy to get word to my family that we had safely arrived at the final camp and were going to make the push to the summit. I was not sure if my message ever made it there.

The unthinkable reality was that I didn't know *for certain* if I was going to make it back. But I viewed that outcome as simply unacceptable. No force in the world was going to keep me from Rachel. Despite the year I'd spent training for this trip, I was completely unprepared for the reality of being on Everest and the toll it would take on me physically. I knew I had to harness every weapon in my physical and spiritual arsenal now. I added a silent mantra with each footstep. *Focus. Step. Pray.* Every inch of progress was a step closer to Rachel and to our future together. For me, that future was worth climbing every massive peak in the Himalayas.

The wind speed continued to increase, and the blasts of blowing snow and ice crystals were now almost constant. When An Doja stopped to unclip his carabiner from the rope at an ice screw and clip it back in on the other side, I turned and looked over my shoulder at the summit. I knew there was just about zero chance of catching a glimpse of Chad and Dave, but every once in a while, I looked anyway.

The summit and most of the mountain above us was no longer visible—all I could see was a swirling wall of clouds and blowing snow. It was like the mountain had disappeared, like there was nothing above me but the sky and the darkening storm.

An Doja was moving again, and I matched his pace, pausing at the same ice screw to move my carabiner around it. The wind changed direction suddenly, now hitting us from behind, so the frozen powder was no longer blowing painfully into my face. The terrain above the Third Step is a steep and exposed snowfield, with very little protection from the full force of the elements. It was at the entrance to this snowfield that we had searched for the ropes on the way up. One small mistake, as simple as placing a foot a few inches in the wrong direction, can mean death.

Planting the crampons of my right boot solidly into the ice, I glanced down the snowy incline on my left and spotted another splash of color. It was another body, limbs splayed out unnaturally. My mind may have been playing tricks on me, but it looked like you could see the path of the fall written in the snow—the outline of the body bracketed by arcs where the climber must have been flailing arms and legs.

*Whoever this climber was, his feet were almost exactly where mine are now just before he slipped.*

That brightly clothed corpse had been a person, someone whose family would never have a body to mourn over or to bury. How long had he been down there? There was no way for me to know. It might have been years. Then again, the accident could have happened only a few hours ago. Much later I would learn that in the several days leading up to and following May 24, a total of six people met their end on Everest, many after summiting.

One climber, known simply as Green Boots, had a permanent place on Everest. In 1996, he was too weak to keep going and took shelter under a rock overhang, eventually dying there. For years afterward, everyone heading for the summit on the northeast route had to pass his body, still curled up with his torso under the ledge and his legs and green boots sticking out toward the trail. What would he have thought of going out like that? If someone had said, "Hey, you can reach the top of Everest, but you won't make it down, and your body will freeze and stay there for years and basically be used as a climbing checkpoint," would Green Boots have thought it was worth it? Without summit fever, I bet he'd have said "heck no" and turned back toward safety.

I had made more than my share of bad judgment calls on the mountain so far. But I'd have plenty of time to beat myself up about it later (I hoped). A gust of wind hit my back with the force of a wrecking ball, then dropped away just as suddenly. Each time that happened, I had to tense every muscle in my body and make myself a statue to avoid being plucked from the face of the mountain.

An Doja's summit earlier in the day had been his sixth. I'd had years of rigorous and grueling physical conditioning and could hold my own against a lot of people, but here on the mountain, I had nothing on An Doja. He seemed superhuman.

For a moment, the wind seemed to die away completely like a protective bubble had popped up around us. As a curtain of blowing snow fell away, I caught a glimpse of ant-sized tents at Camp Three directly below us. This gave me an idea of our progress. We had left the last of the snowfield known as the summit pyramid and were nearing the top of the Second Step, a roughly thirty-foot downward climb of chunky rock. The upper and lower of the three-rock obstacles surrounded the bull's-eye of the notorious Second Step.

*Okay! Keep pushing. The sooner we start down the steps, the sooner we're past them,* I told myself. I resumed my silent mantra.

*Focus. Step. Pray.* Repeat.

Our route angled slightly to the left before the step, and An Doja leaned in toward the steep incline. A ripple moved through the rope to my hand, an echo of An Doja's movement to free a section of rope from the ice. The wind still hadn't returned.

The air was so clear I could see the webbing of An Doja's black harness and the weathered creases of his snowsuit's red fabric. I noticed his left foot come up, higher than it should. Too high. As his leg rose, An Doja reached up and over with his right arm to counterbalance, his hand still clutching the rope. In the time it took me to take a quick, deep inhalation, his body pivoted so that his head and shoulders swung around downslope and his right knee began to buckle.

Before I could exhale, An Doja pitched forward. For a split second, he was falling, frozen in time, his left arm a blur of red against the white backdrop below.

Military instinct kicked in. *Take a knee.* I dropped to a knee, gripping the rope with both hands. Then I tried to make myself an anchor as my partner, guide, and friend toppled off the path toward the snowbank on the edge of Mount Everest slanting seven thousand feet toward the glacier surface below.

# Dancing with Death

**RACHEL**

The sound of a rooster crowing woke me up. I had slept on the second story of a small cement-block building in Guatemala and could see the sun rising. Still snug in Harold's camo military sleeping bag on the hard tile floor, I reached my hand over to where my phone had been charging. No messages.

If my timing was right, Harold should have summited.

*I should probably know something by now.*

My friend Morgan knew I was on edge and asked if I wanted to try to use her phone. She had T-Mobile (just like Harold) and could occasionally catch a signal. I texted both Tommy and Harold from her phone, asking for updates. I was planning on walking to the small internet café next door to check my email, but it didn't open until 8:00 a.m., so I sat waiting, staring at the phone.

Morgan's phone started ringing. It was an 870 number that I didn't recognize, but I picked it up immediately. It didn't connect. I called for Morgan, feeling alarmed, and asked if she knew the number. She didn't but said it could just be a random Guatemala number. I tried to call it back, but the call wouldn't go through.

A few minutes later, a text popped up.

> Have Rachel Earls call this number ASAP.

I started to panic.

*What does this mean? He must be hurt. Something awful has happened.*

I tried to call again, but there was still no answer. My anxiety was rising, and I was barely keeping it together. I texted back

> Calls aren't working, but text is.

No response. The silence was deafening. My mind had now gone to thinking the worst.

I grabbed my wallet and started to head for the door as streams of tears rolled down my face. I was going to try to see if they would let me into the internet café early. Just before leaving, another text came through. I looked at Morgan with fear as she studied her phone.

"Oh no, it's good," she said, handing me the phone. The first three words gave me a huge sense of relief.

> It's your LOML.

This meant "love of my life," a nickname we called each other.

> I was on top of the world this morning, and I'm back at Advanced Base Camp and safe.

The weight of my body released, and I collapsed into Morgan's arms. I had no control in that moment. I just completely lost it.

My mind had gone from thinking the worst to now knowing

Harold was safe. All the weight of the worry I had been carrying around with me was finally gone, and I could breathe again.

Then a voice mail came through. It was from Harold. His voice was the best sound I had ever heard. I smiled and cried at the same time. My hunny was safe and would be coming home to me! A sense of peace came over me as I started to calm down. He went on to say that Chad and Dave were behind him and hadn't made it back to Advanced Camp, so I should be praying for them.

Despite the very unreliable service, I was able to get in contact with Amy, our publicist, and Harold's parents to tell them the news. Then I made my way to the internet café to update social media for everyone following the climb.

It was around 2:00 p.m. the next day when we headed into the town of Antigua and stopped to have some lunch. I connected my phone to the restaurant's Wi-Fi for the first time since being in Guatemala, and suddenly my phone started buzzing and wouldn't stop. Emails and text messages flooded my phone all at once.

Since I'd been running the social media the entire expedition, serving as the main source of communication between Harold and the world, everyone had been trying to reach me. By that point, they all knew more than I did.

It was an influx of confusion as I tried to piece together what actually happened up there on that mountain. As far as I knew, Harold was safe and healthy. That's all he had told me, and I had no reason to think otherwise. Then I read a *USA Today* article saying that Harold had suffered bloody, frostbitten toes."[*]

As I read the article, these words and phrases ran through my head: *frostbite, lost goggles, snow blind,* and *falling off a ledge.* I sat at the end of the table, my eyes glued to my phone, and completely lost it

---

[*] Gregg Zoroya, "Ex-Soldier Who Lost a Leg in Iraq Reaches the Top of Everest," *USA Today,* May 24, 2016, www.usatoday.com/story/news/world/2016/05/24/ex-soldier-who-lost-leg-iraq-reaches-top-everest/84860106.

again. I must have made everyone feel so uncomfortable while they were trying to eat, but I had nowhere else to go. I couldn't walk outside or I'd lose the connection.

May 25, 2016

RACHEL: I'm just now reading all these updates.

AMY (with Pitch Publicity): I talked to Harold on the phone today. He said his feet were beat up, but it wasn't too bad, and he can climb down with no problem. He sounded really good.

RACHEL: You promise? I'm nervous he isn't telling all the truth not to scare me since he didn't tell me anything.

AMY: I'm telling you the truth. I don't know if he's telling me the truth. But he did sound good.

My world flipped upside down in those moments. The relief of feeling that he was safe had just been taken away from me. I'd heard his voice, so I knew he was alive, but what else wasn't he telling me? Why hadn't he told me *any* of the other details? I felt like he was hiding information to protect me, and I had no real way of getting the full story until I saw him in person.

## HAROLD

When An Doja tripped and fell off the narrow path, I thought he very well could have fallen seven thousand feet and joined the bodies below. And maybe taken me with him.

The rope connecting us, secured by ice screws in the rock face, became taut from the weight of his body. I dropped to my knee and tried to hold the rope, but I don't think it actually helped, as the ice screws were still in place. I remember feeling the sensation of the rope catching, and he fell just a few feet into a snow slope right off the path. The ropes held. I can't describe the look we gave each other; it felt like it lasted an eternity, although it was just a split second. He didn't say anything and neither did I, but we both knew death had been as close as it can be without winning.

He quickly climbed back to a secure spot on the ledge off the steep snow slope, and we both took a breather while the winds howled and picked up speed. Later, we learned that wind gusts were reaching seventy-five to eighty miles per hour. The noise was deafening.

It would have been easy to become crippled with fear, but my military training helped. Whenever you experience or see something that might be hard to take in, like the close call with my Sherpa or the sight of the dead climbers, you can't hesitate. You see it, take it in, and press forward. An Doja and I were a buddy team, a fire team as we call it in the military, and it was our job to take care of each other.

My strength was depleted, and I felt weaker and weaker, like my stomach bug was returning and zapping any remaining energy. We started the final descent toward Camp Three, fighting our way through the winds, unable to see much. Snow was blowing up underneath the sunglasses I'd borrowed from An Doja. My hand was freezing because I'd also lost a mitten and had only the liner. I tried keeping that hand balled up into a fist as much as possible to prevent my fingers from getting frostbite.

We kept pushing downward. Right after the Second Step, I noticed I was extremely tired and dizzy. I felt drunk. I was losing my balance. I didn't know it, but my body was craving oxygen, and as a result, I was quickly fading.

"Your tank is no good," An Doja yelled above the wind. It was empty. He quickly replaced my tank and turned up the flow. An immediate jolt of life sprang back into me as I was pumped with Os. *Wow! I love oxygen*, I thought.

It was like a resurrection of sorts, renewing my determination to get down the mountain. We gathered some steam as we got lower in altitude, out of the death zone, increasing the level of oxygen in our blood. We made just quick stops at the upper camps before pressing on to Advanced Base Camp.

Camp Two was a wasteland by the time we got there. The storm was on top of us and had blown away nearly all the tents. Polls sticking in the ground were the only remnants of an orange tent city that once existed. We found one of the only remaining tents and climbed in as the winds ferociously shook it. We needed a break from the storm. We were physically depleted and sucking bad. A Sherpa came by and said, "You must keep moving! It's not safe here!" We pressed on, my body in agony and utterly depleted of energy.

I didn't know it at the time, but my toe had gotten frostbitten from the time I had spent sitting outside my tent at Camp Three, waiting to depart for the summit. All I knew was that my feet were burning in pain. When we finally made it down, I felt like we'd been gone forever.

I saw Tommy standing outside his tent and mustered up the energy to yell his name. He looked over at us, appearing confused, not making out who we were. He hadn't expected us to come down so quickly. We were supposed to spend the night at Camp One or Camp Two, but the weather was so bad we just kept pressing downward to safety. We had climbed from Camp Three to the summit and then back down, passing Camps Three, Two, and One, all the way to Advanced Base Camp in about thirty-six hours of straight climbing and no sleep. We had been dancing with death.

Tommy and I gave each other a huge hug. He handed me a Coca-Cola, which was a rarity in this remote area. I sat down and took my boots off to find my feet bloody and toenails missing. Not surprising, given I'd descended nine thousand feet with my toes ramming the front of my steel boots. Strangely, my big toe wasn't bleeding but was stone white.


May 25, 2016

RACHEL: Harold got frostbite?!
KIRBY: Frostnip! I think! Not as bad.
RACHEL: What!!! He almost went blind?! And fell off a ridge?

KIRBY: Yeah, apparently! The Sherpa that H was tied to almost fell 7,000 feet, but Harold grabbed the rope and the rope caught after about 10 feet.

RACHEL: OMG. I don't know if I should know any of this.

KIRBY: Harold is fine now! We were worried for a while because we didn't hear from him from the time he left Advanced Base Camp until he returned after summiting.

RACHEL: This is horrifying.

Same day

RACHEL'S MOM: Have you talked to H? Chad and Dave are not back yet. So extremely thankful H and the rest of the team are at ABC, but praying for Dave and Chad.

RACHEL: What? Isn't everyone safe? I see now Chad and Dave aren't back.

RACHEL'S MOM: No. Dave got a stomach bug on the climb up. The team ended up separated.

RACHEL: I see now. OMG! I can't handle all this.

RACHEL'S MOM: Harold summitted at 7:40 a.m. and then Chad and Dave at 8:35 a.m.

RACHEL: I can't believe everything that happened to Harold.

RACHEL'S MOM: Harold then booked it hard back to ABC. Exhausting descent, but he made it. Dave and Chad made it down to Camp Three. It was a bad storm and getting worse, but thankfully they made it there. They were originally expected to make it to ABC by dinnertime, but they had to stop higher up the mountain.

RACHEL: Gosh, I'm praying. I'm really thankful I wasn't home for this because I can't handle it. This is really hard to process right now.

## HAROLD

I had been trying to reach Rachel from my satellite phone but couldn't get ahold of her. My heart broke knowing she was sitting by the phone, distraught and anxious, desperate to hear my voice.

I texted Rachel's friend and told her to call me ASAP. I wanted

Rachel to hear the good news straight from my voice, not through a measly text! After I was able to let Rachel know I was safe, I chatted with Tommy and other teammates about the last point on the mountain where we had seen Chad and Dave. Other climbers from our team had made it back ahead of me, but Dave and Chad were still behind me. It became clear no one had any idea where they were on the mountain or if they were okay. The gravity of our team's communication mistake really began sinking its teeth into me.

Even as calls began coming in from ABC News and *Good Morning America*, I had two members of our team still out there on the mountain. My stomach was in knots, and I felt numb with exhaustion. The anxiety was so intense I stepped out of my tent to throw up. There are no words to adequately describe the weight of emotion you experience with the knowledge that because of your bad decision, someone might die and you have no way to remedy the situation.

Our publicist, Amy, was getting calls from a variety of media. Having just gotten off the mountain, I felt physically drained and emotionally vulnerable. I didn't realize it then, but I definitely was not prepared to begin telling our story. I took the call with ABC News while in my sleeping bag, trying to get warm. It was a decision I would instantly regret, as we still had two climbers on the mountain getting pounded by a storm while I was back in the comfort of my sleeping bag, talking to the media about our summit and cause.

In hindsight, talking to the media at that point was an immature act and not something expected from a leader and teammate. I should have been doing everything in my power to figure out how to communicate with Dave and Chad. Even worse, during the interview, I let the journalist steer the conversation away from our cause and to my rough descent and the storm. Normally, I was good at keeping the messaging on point with our awareness cause so that the story remained about our cause and not about us. But when the story broke, it was headlined "US Soldiers Recount Harrowing Descent from Mt. Everest" and mentioned virtually nothing about our cause and those we were trying to help.

The reporter also exacerbated small, intense details of the story, freaking out my family back home. Then I made matters worse by saying "That's what we learn in the military. You don't ever leave a Soldier behind. It's the same thing with Sherpa" in reference to An Doja and me sticking together.* I felt like a hypocrite after the call. I told Amy to cancel the rest of the media calls for the time being.

Radio chatter between Sherpas revealed that Chad and Dave were spending the night at Camp Three, then heading down the next day. The Sherpa on the other end came over the net and said, "Oh no, that's not good. It's really bad up there." They were still in the death zone getting pounded by even stronger winds than those An Doja and I had faced.

NORAD, the North American Aerospace Defense Command, was supplying us with weather data and predicted the winds to be hurricane force, reaching one hundred miles an hour. I walked out of my tent and looked up toward the summit, which you can normally see clearly even at night, but it was black, as though there wasn't even a mountain present. She was engulfed in the rage of the storm.

By now, it was the next day. No updates. Climbers and Sherpas were staggering into camp with frostbitten limbs and fluid in their lungs. It looked as if the mountain had chewed them up and spit them out.

The ABC News article broke and caused a whirlwind back home with our family. Rachel was freaking out because I had talked to her just that one time to tell her I had made it back to Advanced Camp and had shared nothing more. Chad's mom was livid, and for

---

* Morgan Winsor, "US Soldiers Recount Harrowing Descent from Mt. Everest," ABC News, May 26, 2016, https://abcnews.go.com/International/us-soldiers-recount-harrowing-descent-mt-everest/story?id=39399897.

good reason. How could I make a comment like that with her son still on the mountain? And though I was referring to my Sherpa and me, she was right. We should have either had better communication plans or stayed together. We had done neither. Unfortunately, Rachel, as our social media liaison, was taking the brunt of all this as the link between our team and the families.

## RACHEL

I was surprised to find out Chad and Dave still hadn't made it back, and I was starting to worry. I tried my best to process what had happened and what was still going on as I reached out to the other climbers' families. It was a hard place to be in because I didn't know why they had gotten separated up on the mountain. But, understandably so, some of the family members were taking their frustration and worries out on me over the failed communication that happened on the climb. Nevertheless, I was just the messenger.

I was basically having to stand up for my husband when I myself didn't know what the reasoning was at the time. I was already so emotional from learning about the frostbite and the dangers my husband went through; it was a lot to process, plus having the weight of the other families' emotions on me.

I think there was confusion with the families of the other climbers about what my job was as the one running social media. My role was to post on social media and communicate with our publicist. Often, Amy and I had conflicting opinions about what info to share and when. It was never my role to be in direct contact with the climbers' friends or family members, although looking back, someone should have had that role. We just assumed each climber would communicate back home with their family.

Over Facebook Messenger, I explained my best guess as to what had happened in an effort to help make sense of the situation.

I can only imagine if they went down the mountain
earlier it is because they needed to. It isn't safe for
anyone to stay up that high for any amount of time
and it would have been harder on the team if everyone
stayed, increasing the chance of more people getting
hurt and not being able to get down. What I mean is,
I think it would have been worse for everyone because
if they were all to get hurt no one could help anyone.
Also, from the very beginning I was told that everyone
climbs at a different pace, and so everyone is essentially climbing alone or just with their Sherpa. Before
all of this I thought they climbed as a team too, but it
became clear that just isn't practical or safe since their
bodies are all different and some climbers would either
have to slow down for the others or speed up instead of
climbing at a healthy pace for their bodies.

The news of Harold summiting was nothing like I'd expected
it to be. Instead of celebrating this big accomplishment, I felt like
everything had come crashing down. Families were angry, and I was
terrified of what I didn't know.

## HAROLD

By 2:00 a.m., I was completely exhausted, yet I felt this overwhelming guilt that I'd failed as a teammate. I called my dad from the
satellite phone and summed up the situation.

"I'm contemplating going back up to find them."

To be honest, I expected my father to respond by saying that I
should stay safe and pray for my teammates or maybe try checking
at the international camps, which I had already done. What he actually said cut me to the core and is probably the single most impact-
ful advice I've ever received, especially since I know how difficult it
was for him to give.

"Son," came his voice over the line, "you need to head back up that mountain and back into the storm, even if it kills you. Because that is what leaders do. Whether you are the climbing leader or not, you are responsible for those men, and that means you don't leave them out there on their own. You need to find them or die trying."

I could hear him fighting back tears, and I felt a deep sadness rise in my chest. I don't remember exactly what I said next, but we both knew the gravity of my father's words. We both understood that he may have just given his only son advice that would send him to his grave. We were both in tears as I told my father goodbye.

With frostbitten feet and bags under my eyes, I started prepping to go back out into the unforgiving elements and the eye of the storm. I was terrified, but I knew it was the right thing to do.

# Homecoming

**HAROLD**

I was in the mess tent scarfing down donkey sausage and eggs as I prepared to head back up the mountain. At this point, we'd heard that Dave and Chad were at Camp One, but we weren't sure if that was actually true because we had been playing a game of telephone with Sherpas from other camps and with whatever communication equipment they had up on the mountain.

Then I heard the news: Dave and Chad had been spotted at the bottom of the North Col, about thirty minutes from Advanced Camp. I burst out of the tent, leaving my plate of half-eaten sausage, and walked as fast as I could to meet them. I tried to jog, but that didn't last long at twenty thousand feet on jagged glacial rocks with wounded feet.

I was excited and relieved but still on edge until I could see them for myself and know they were all right. Then I saw them. I ran to them and gave them huge hugs. They had half smiles on their faces and were pretty banged up, but most important, they were alive. Chad had frostbite on all his fingers, and they were bubbling with blisters. Despite the treacherous journey, shortly after returning to the tent, I could see their infectious smiles and personalities shine through again. They had a resiliency unlike any I'd seen before. When we all encircled them, asking about the weather on the descent, all Dave said was, "It was really bad, man."*

Our team slowly worked our way off the mountain. We had more than a weeklong journey back to our families. I was heading home to the love of my life, who was waiting for me. She was all I could think about. I'd had a dangerous love affair with a mountain that almost took me away from my wife, and coming out on the other side, I just wanted to see her warm smile and wrap her in my arms.

Every day, as I flew closer to seeing her—Tibet, Nepal, Qatar, Atlanta—I got more and more giddy. The kind of giddy where I would randomly smile while sitting by myself on the plane because I was daydreaming about her. Plus, the plane had free on-demand movies, so you can bet I was watching *The Notebook* on repeat. Our story was about to have its happy ending.

**RACHEL**

The news of Chad and Dave's return was a huge relief, although emotions remained high. Chad's mom made a joke about how he might be grounded after this. We all recognized that things could have easily been so much worse, and we were now just ready for our loved ones to be safe at home. After two long, emotionally taxing months of being separated from Harold, I waited for him at the airport. In my hands were the two Welcome Home posters I had made. My legs fidgeted as I stood waiting with the rest of his family.

As soon as I spotted him, I started running. He was moving so slowly. I could tell it was uncomfortable for him to walk due to his frostbitten toe, but he was slower than a turtle. It took him forever

* Watch Dave in the midst of the storm at Earls.org/descent.

to pass that red Do Not Cross line at the terminal before I could hug him. He had a scruffy beard and greasy long hair, and he was super skinny.

Waiting for him to get to me felt like the same "come on!" moment before the pastor said "You can now kiss your bride!" on our wedding day.

## HAROLD

The automatic double doors leaving the terminal opened, and I saw her. It felt like our wedding day all over again, except this time I was the one making the long walk down the aisle. There she was, standing with all my family and holding huge signs. I started walking slowly because I wanted to soak it all in. I also had my foot bandaged and was pushing two huge duffel bags.

"Hunny!" Rachel called out as she jumped up and down, waiting for me to cross the line. "Hurry up! Hurry up!"

I dropped the bags when she jumped into my arms.

"I've missed you so much," Rachel said, and her hug felt stronger than usual.

"I love you," I said as I finally was able to see her up close. I'd missed that smile so much.

"I'm so glad you're home."

Before she could say anything more, I kissed her. We embraced once again, and then Rachel showed me the posters she'd made for me. As she did, my momma ran up to me and gave me a huge hug with tears in her eyes. (I feel like all moms cry at this point in the story.) My dad came up to me, embraced me, and said, "Son, I'm proud of you. Welcome home!"**

We were all going to have lunch together at a restaurant, but the moment Rachel and I got in the car, I just wanted to soak up my time with her. She was so patient in sharing me with my family,

** Watch the video of us reuniting in the airport at Earls.org/Homecoming.

but I knew deep down all she really wanted was time just for us. If I'd had my way, we would have gotten takeout and headed home to continue our reunion.

After we were full of food and stories, we finally made it home. Our dogs went nuts seeing me walk through the back door again. I had to put my foot up on a chair so they wouldn't accidentally step on my damaged toe. They were jumping and making all kinds of weird excited noises, shaking their butts, and spinning around. They licked my face about fifty times!

I later went to the kitchen and grabbed a warm bowl of water to soak my foot. My white toe had now turned completely purple. I would be leaving for Ranger School fewer than two months after summiting Mount Everest. I knew I had to act fast and do everything I could to treat my toe in time. I hoped I wouldn't lose it, but only time would tell.

Two weeks later, I had an Army doctor from Fort Benning, Georgia, check it out. He said, "I must be honest. I've never seen frostbite like this before. I think we're going to have to take off your toe." I got a second opinion. The next doctor said the toe should heal within about a year but there would be nerve damage. The good news: I got to keep my toe, but any sort of impact was painful. Dancing or even lifting my foot out of bed was a delicate process. My whole toenail turned black and purple and eventually fell off. I saved the toenail and eventually gave it to my cousin Ryan as a Christmas present in a nice ring display box.

### RACHEL

Whoa, whoa, *whoa* there, buddy! He might have given it to Ryan as a joke, but he didn't let him keep it! That nasty thing is still in our home because he won't let me throw it out! Harold will tell you it is now a family heirloom!

Just one week after Harold got back from Everest, we celebrated our one-year wedding anniversary! I hadn't always been sure we would spend this special day together, so it felt really good to wake up next to each other. Time has a wonderful way of showing us what really matters. We begin to appreciate the time we have when we're aware we could easily lose it. Every time we've been apart has made us more appreciative of the time we have together, and we end up loving harder and living a fuller life.

The morning of our first anniversary, I woke Harold up with breakfast in bed. We had biscuits with gravy, eggs, and bacon in an attempt to replicate our favorite breakfast place in New York City: Jacob's Pickles. We ate every last bite while we cuddled and reflected on how insane the past year had been and how much we had grown together.

It was hard to come up with our favorite memories because we had so many! In that year alone, we had gone to eighteen countries together (and several separately), moved twice, gotten two dogs, and started a nonprofit to help veterans. I'd built a YouTube channel, and Harold had climbed Everest! Who knew where life might take us? Maybe we'd have kids soon! No matter what was going to happen in the next year, we were just excited to be able to do life together.

## HAROLD

I wanted kids. Like yesterday.

The day after I returned from Everest, we left the house early to head to Atlanta for two Everest-related interviews. I was grateful to the media for their interest and for the opportunity to bring awareness to PTSD, but the continued effort was taking a toll on both Rachel and me as we struggled to adjust our sleeping patterns and get back to our normal life.

The media interviews went well, but they portrayed our expedition as a total success. From the outside it was, but they didn't know about the unjustifiable risks we had taken. The poor decisions made in the extreme elements that caused us to get split up on the mountain had a huge impact on me as a leader. Not one of the 278 media outlets featuring our climb ever knew how bad things had gotten and the poor decisions I'd made as a young leader. My hope is that someone reading this book can grow as a person and leader, as I have, by learning from my failures.

I learned so many things on that mountain, especially on that final night. I learned that communication can be the difference between life and death; that when you are in pivotal moments, you must clearly communicate and keep things simple to understand. I learned that when I am tired, I am vulnerable to mishaps. Which means I need to take a tactical pause, rest, and then recenter and reengage. I learned that although our mission comes first (raising awareness for PTSD), it shouldn't be at the expense of the team. I learned that as the youngest and least experienced member of my seasoned team, I can always use common sense to help bridge the gap left by the experience I don't have. I learned that it is harder to sit and wait helplessly to find out if your loved one is alive or dead than it is to climb the highest mountain in the world.

I also learned, as Rachel told me later, that you can't just ask God to save the person you love most and leave it at that. This kind of prayer relies only on one-way communication. Instead, Rachel taught me through her own example that you must fully put your faith in God to carry you through the worst, no matter the outcome. That is the essence of true communication with God. It's the definition of faith in its purest form.

I will carry these lessons with me and rely on them as I continue to grow as a leader, husband, and person.

A few days after the media interviews, we had a big welcome-home party at Zac Brown's Southern Ground, inviting sponsors, media, and other people important to the USX effort. I got up to speak and thanked everyone who helped us make Everest a success. Well, not everyone. I thanked a lot of people, but there was one I didn't: Rachel. She didn't need the recognition, but I hadn't even acknowledged she was part of the team.

Of course I appreciated her, but for a while after Everest, I failed to recognize all she had done and sacrificed for me, for us, and for our future family. She was the only reason I was able to climb Everest, yet I hadn't even given her so much as a thank-you. She went with me to all the interviews and helped me prepare. She helped launch USX. She did all the social media, and she was still crushing her own passions on the side.

It took Rachel calling me out to finally realize this.

I already knew that when you're a leader, those you love will naturally have to make sacrifices. But it took growing closer to God and getting away from my egotistical self to fully appreciate what others, especially Rachel, had done to help me along the way.

Right after I stood up and talked, CSM Burnett got up and shared his struggles with suicidal thoughts. His honesty made an impact on everyone there. It was a profound moment and made the mission real for me again, reinforcing why we'd climbed.

## RACHEL

CSM Burnett talked about how PTSD affected not only his life but also his family's life. He also thanked his wife, Antoinette, for being by his side through everything. I sat at our table with tears dripping from my eyes because I could relate. Harold didn't fully realize what family members go through, but I did.

All along I felt like there was a voice not being heard as we spoke about PTSD: the voice of the spouses and family members. I married an infantry officer, which means there is a very strong probability that he'll someday go to combat. Never once would Harold consider that he might come back with PTSD because he can't go in with that mentality.

On the other hand, as his wife, I have had that concern from the very beginning. Is he going to change? What would that mean for our marriage? Is he going to be closed off? I knew Everest could have effects similar to those of PTSD from combat.

That's why I cared so much about the expedition. I didn't have PTSD and my husband didn't have PTSD, but the possibility of it affecting my life was certainly real. The fact that it does affect many military families was real to me. I just wished it was talked about more from the perspective of the families.

Even if our Soldiers don't end up with PTSD, we as spouses live with that concern. It's the fear of the person you love more than anything going through something you can't do anything about. Watching the person you love the most struggle and knowing you can't really help him . . . that's what so many spouses and family members experience.

To be honest, we were in a bit of a funk as we tried to transition back into our normal life. I was going full force with my vlogs, posting a new video nearly every day. Harold wasn't used to being home all day and having to do normal tasks around the house, like sweeping or washing dishes. This led to some arguments, as he didn't take too well to this change in roles.

Our failure came in not discussing what his being home more would look like. Harold felt like he wasn't as productive as he wanted to be because he was having to stop what he was doing to take the dogs out to potty. What he didn't realize was that I was always at home. I had to juggle all the normal housework and take care of the dogs while also managing to do my own work.

It caused some friction, but our arguments never lasted long because we can't stand to be upset with each other. We talked it out, and it ended up being a necessary and eye-opening conversation. We knew if we wanted to bring kids into our new family, the level of responsibility was going to skyrocket for both of us and we needed to figure all this out beforehand. Bottom line: he was going to have to step up a lot. If we had just talked about our changing roles in advance, we could have avoided that whole argument.

## HAROLD

Rachel actually told me during one of our arguments that we weren't ready for kids because I wasn't being the husband and partner I needed to be. This hurt because I have always wanted to be a father, but she was right. I wasn't being a team player. If it didn't have to do with what I wanted or was working on, then I wouldn't do it. It sounds pathetic, and it was, but I needed to mature as a man and as a partner in our relationship. I was getting mad at her for things she wasn't doing for me, never once thinking about the things I should be doing for her.

We eventually sat down to have a heart-to-heart, and we decided to start doing things for each other to show we care. One night, Rachel made me a handwritten card that she taped on the door so I'd see it before I left for work, addressed to "my sweet, funny, extra handsome, loving, kind, goofy, passionate, hardworking, God-fearing husband." She also put a sticky note on my box of Krave cereal that said, "I Krave you all the time ☺." I bought her flowers (well, actually, I picked them from the yard of a neighbor who'd just moved), put them in the vase I brought her from Tibet, set out the flowers and a banana for when she woke up, and wrote her a letter.

Transition periods, reunions, and reintegration can often be some of the most challenging times in a relationship, and I think it all boils down to expectations. We often expect that the moment we're reunited with our loved one, everything will easily fall into place again. We've naturally built it up in our mind, forgetting that one or both people probably feel physically, mentally, and emotionally exhausted.

Something Rachel and I have learned is that if you aren't feeling the love from your spouse, there is a good chance you aren't giving it either. When you start to intentionally do things out of love, there is a good chance that love will be returned.

# Ranger School

**HAROLD**

Research shows that it takes the human body six months to an entire year to recover from Everest. Fewer than two months after climbing Everest, I planned to go to Ranger School. Ranger School is one of the toughest schools in the military, designed to break your body down physically. It includes moving through swamps carrying rucksacks weighing more than one hundred pounds and enduring exhaustion and sleep deprivation. The goal is to push your body further than it thinks it can go.

The first week is called RAP week, which stands for Ranger Assessment Phase. Basically, it's meant to assess your physical stamina and mental toughness and ends with a twelve-mile ruck march, in which you carry almost fifty pounds on your back. You have to complete the event in a certain amount of time; if you don't, you fail and go home.

My body was still in a weakened condition. While I had regained most of my weight, my body didn't feel or perform the same. I was still dealing with nerve damage in my foot from frostbite, and I prayed my body would hold up.

## RACHEL

As we got back in sync, I did my best to help Harold prepare for Ranger School. I made checklists of all the gear he needed, helped him pack, and went on runs with him so he could practice rucking. We'd done this before when he was training for Everest, but this time, the backpack Harold was carrying was heavier and camouflaged.

Meanwhile, I was trying to prepare myself for his absence again. He'd been gone for two months for Everest, been home for fewer than two months, and was about to leave again for anywhere from two to six months. As much as I didn't want to acknowledge it, the upcoming separation was inevitable. He soon laced up his military ACU boots for the first time since his frostbite. Then he shaved his head with no guard on the clippers (hello, Baldy!), which is the standard haircut for Ranger School.

My goal this time while Harold was gone was to simply be happy and do things to stay busy, just not as extreme as before. I knew Ranger School was going to be trying, but at least it wasn't life threatening like Everest, right? I didn't know how dangerous it actually was until the first week.

This time around, I'd made friends with my neighbors and felt a sense of community. Even though I'd have hardly any communication with Harold, I knew he was relatively close by instead of being on the other side of the world. That made me feel good.

A couple of days after Harold left, I got a message from a person in the military community that someone at Ranger School had passed away. As I read those words, I felt every single emotion. It was heartbreaking. Second Lt. Michael R. Parros was treated for hyponatremia (low sodium in the body) at the hospital but did not make it. I was heartbroken for his family and loved ones. This brought the realization to the forefront of my mind of just how dangerous the military lifestyle is. I didn't know if Harold knew him or if he had been present when it happened. My mind was all over

the place. All I could do was pray for peace that surpasses all understanding. I was prepared (as much as I could be) for the possibility
of Harold's death on Everest, but his going into Ranger School was
supposed to bring a sense of relief. Now it didn't. All I wanted to do
was talk to Harold.

## HAROLD

I was actually doing push-ups and other physical exercises all day
right next to Mike (2LT Parros). He was in great shape and had
been a fellow athlete at West Point, so we were drawn to each other
due to our similar backgrounds. We encouraged each other when
we'd pass by during physical events. It was heartbreaking to lose a
fellow Ranger buddy.

The following day was eerily somber as we silently did push-
ups while the Ranger instructors' hollering fell on deaf ears. The
tragedy of Mike's passing left me with the gripping realization of
just how hard Ranger School could be, and it gave me an enormous
amount of self-doubt. How could I pass Ranger School, much less
the ruck march—a final test of grit and physical stamina—when my
body was still not even close to recovered from climbing at twenty-
nine-thousand feet just weeks earlier?

I normally would have approached the twelve-mile ruck with
confidence, but now I felt uneasy because of the quick turnaround
after Everest. I had been cleared by the doctor to start working out
again just one week before Ranger School. I had considered de-
laying Ranger School until the winter, but I hadn't been allowed
to since they deemed my frostbite a cold-weather injury. My only
option was to go to Ranger School right away, despite the further
recovery my body needed.

## RACHEL

The night I knew Harold was doing the twelve-mile ruck was long.
Come morning, Harold called me. I knew immediately what his call

meant. In Ranger School, no news is good news. I wasn't supposed to hear from him until the end of the week, so his call meant he had failed the ruck. Even though it was a bad cell connection, I could tell from the sound of his voice that he was devastated. Normally, he'd be sent home immediately, but because of the death, they were holding Soldiers while an investigation took place.

I was hurting for him and I knew he was beating himself up, but I also knew he hadn't been physically ready. I spent the whole day waiting and never got a call again. I finally went to sleep at 4:00 a.m. I wondered what the failure meant for us. I felt bad that he was stuck there waiting, surrounded by all things Ranger School, a constant reminder of his failure. Would we be moving again? Or would he go back to Ranger School for a second try? All I knew was I wanted to hug him.

Everything was hitting me so hard. I could feel the weight of all we'd been through recently. But failure is inevitable, and I knew it was something we could get through together. We'd come out even tougher, gaining wisdom along the way. As I thought about Harold, his personality, and his achievements, I thought how sometimes failure can be harder on those who are experiencing it for the first time. If you're successful in most things, defeat can feel overwhelming because you're not accustomed to losing. I didn't want that to happen.

When Harold came home, he immediately spoke with his command and found out he would be going back to Ranger School on August 22, which was in about three weeks. His face was covered in pimples that looked like a bunch of tiny ant bites because he hadn't showered and was constantly covered in dirt and sweat. He took that first day at home to rest, then immediately started training for the ruck again. He was more determined than ever.

## HAROLD

The two hardest phone calls of my life were both with Rachel. The first was when I called her from Everest after I got sick. The second was when I called her from Ranger School to tell her I failed the ruck. I had never failed anything physical in my entire life, and it was humiliating.

I was embarrassed that after an achievement like climbing Mount Everest, I couldn't pass the first week of Ranger School. Whether I was successful or not, God had a plan for it all. I realized that I not only needed to get back in physical shape (and cut out the waffles and brownie batter) but also needed the right mind-set if I was going to be ready to go back in three weeks. I still carried the failure, and it was depleting my already ravaged mind and body. The only way I have ever had any real success is by fully committing to and immersing myself in what I wanted to do.

Rachel and I ate, slept, and focused on Ranger School for all hours of the day for three weeks. Ruck at 5:00 a.m. Lean breakfast. Motivational Ranger video. Knot-tying class while taking a shower. Reciting the Ranger creed on full blast with the windows down in the car while driving to dinner. Then a workout after that. Rachel punching my stomach repeatedly as I did crunches while hanging from a pull-up bar with my shirt off. Just kidding about the Rocky Balboa moment. But if I learned one thing about Rachel and me with Everest, it was that if together we wholeheartedly set our minds on achieving something we believe in, we are unstoppable.

## RACHEL

After a sleepless night full of nerves and anxiety, I woke up and headed to the kitchen to prepare one final breakfast. It was the first day of Ranger School, round two, and the third goodbye we'd share in the span of five months. As I type this right now, I want to pat myself on the back for how much of a boss I was for getting through all this. If there is one thing I want readers to take away from our story, it is that you are capable of more than you can imagine and that with God by your side, you will always come out stronger!

Harold threw his two huge green duffel bags in the back of our car, and we drove to the drop-off point. He looked better, felt better, and had a determined look on his face as he slung his 120 pounds of gear on his back. I knew he was ready when he walked away with a smile. That was the Harold I knew. Instead of leaving with a bad attitude, reluctant to get right back "in the suck," as Soldiers call it, he was ready to crush it.

## HAROLD

Well . . . I was mostly ready, but I naturally still had some nervous thoughts racing in my mind. Ranger School was a time when I had to lean on God because I didn't want to fail again. I knew my faith was more up and down than Rachel's, and I sometimes chased after God only when I needed Him.

Everest brought me closer to God during the difficult times on the mountain, but after it was all over, my interest waned. I'd jammed to worship music on the way to Everest, but on the way home, I jammed to hip-hop. I prayed my way up and down the mountain but forgot to pray back at home, except at the dinner table. I realized I had an underlying belief that I didn't always need God because I believed He would get in the way of what I wanted to accomplish.

This time my heart felt different.

## RACHEL

Two days after Harold left, I hit over a million views on my YouTube channel. Although I couldn't celebrate with Harold, I kept thinking how grateful I was for his continued support and encouragement. By Wednesday night, there was no news from Harold, so I knew he had made it through the first few days again and would be starting that dreaded twelve-mile ruck in just a few short hours. I couldn't sleep, so I covered him in prayers.

> *Lord, You have called him here; now use him how You please.*
> *May he be an encouraging ear, a battle buddy, and more as You*
> *use his strengths to lift him up and show him his purpose. I pray*

*for friendship and conversation that take his mind off the pain.*
*I pray for radical healing in his weak muscles and for health, a*
*positive attitude, and a hopeful heart. May You turn those lonely*
*hours into beautiful moments with You, Lord. Give these Soldiers*
*the power, strength, and mental fortitude they need to get through*
*this.*

Around 10:00 a.m., I felt peace because I knew that no matter what happened, God would work through the situation. We'd
been separated by the mountain and come out with a fiercer love
and deeper appreciation for life, so I knew we could get through
anything together. I'd be there if he needed me, or I'd celebrate
him if he didn't. By noon, still no news. By 3:00 p.m., still no call,
which meant *he had done it*! I literally had a party, jumping on the
bed with the dogs and dancing in the kitchen. I was so proud! I
had that same excited feeling I had when I got the text message
that Harold had arrived at Base Camp for the first time. I lived
in the moment and felt the emotions I knew Harold was having
when he'd finished that ruck: proud, fired up, and confident. I
even ate some cake in celebration since I could eat cake but Harold couldn't.

## HAROLD

I absolutely crushed the ruck march. I made some good friends, and
we stuck together the entire time. We laughed and shared stories,
including my Princess Jasmine story. This helped take our minds
off the misery and heavy weight on our backs. We actually had a
few other Rangers link up with us because they were sucking pretty
bad and needed some encouragement. One of them pulled me aside
afterward and said, "Because of you, I was able to pass. Thank you."
It was pitch black out. I couldn't see his face and never got his name,
but his comment really meant a lot to me.

No one ever wants to fail, but in hindsight, I was grateful for my initial failure. It was a crushing blow to my pride. From it, however, I grew so much as a person, leader, and husband. Most important, it caused me to reflect on the type of person I was on the home front. I mentioned earlier that while growing up, Tommy and I always lived by the Andy Stanley quote "Start becoming the person the person you're looking for is looking for." So why did that mentality stop being my focus once I got married? I decided from then on to be the person the person I'm married to wants to be married to.

## RACHEL

I had sent Harold a set of prestamped and addressed envelopes just in case he had time to write to me. One day, sitting in my mailbox was a little piece of gold, a letter from Harold. It was a week old by the time I received it.

*Aug 28th*

*Dear hunny,*

*I think about you often . . . Also, since you didn't get a call, you already know this, but I passed the ruck! Ha ha, I laughed out loud at your letter . . .*

One of the letters I'd sent Harold was labeled "open before the ruck." I'd kept it simple and to the point, with big letters that said, "PASS THE RUCK." In the letter, he talked about some funny stuff from Ranger School. He said he had gone three straight days with no sleep and had never hallucinated so much in his life. He would jump over creeks that didn't exist or try to sit down on his ruck that wasn't there. And he fell over three times from falling asleep while standing up.

Fast-forward a little bit. Harold was now in the third and final phase of Ranger School: swamp phase. I received another letter.

This one contained a prayer.

> *Dear God,*
>
> *Rachel and I come to You today to praise You for who You are. We can't thank You enough for Your love toward us and our love we share together. I've been blessed with the most beautifully created woman, inside and out, and she is a great reflection of You. God, I pray that although we are not together physically, our love for each other continues to grow stronger. I feel so blessed right now, God, and I feel like You have a plan for everything. Please take care of and protect my wife in my absence. God, we love You, we want You in our lives, and we pray You will use us in a grand and mighty way. We love You, God. In Your name, amen.*

I could see an obvious spiritual growth happening in him, reflected in the letters he sent me. I was so sure climbing Everest would bring him closer to God, but as it turns out, it wasn't until after Everest and a few more challenges that he was able to see how clearly God was working in his life. It was a good reminder for me that we all walk our own road with God. While I can support and encourage those around me in their faith, it isn't fair to put a timeline or expectations on someone else's walk.

## HAROLD

At Ranger School, the chaplain handed out a devotional book to every Ranger. My squad mates and I would pull it out while lying in a swamp on security duty, read it, and then talk about it for hours. It reminded me of the value of having a friend to talk with about God. I was constantly learning new stuff about God and my faith. The difference between Ranger School and Everest was that now I was intentionally working on my faith. On Everest, I was simply touching base with God, making sure He could hear me with a "hey, look at me, I'm worshipping You" kind of mind-set because I wanted Him close. On Everest, I wanted God close to me; at Ranger School, I wanted to be close to God.

Looking back, I realize that I took for granted how strong Rachel's relationship was with God and used it as an excuse for thinking, *Oh, she'll be fine.* I hadn't done anything to help her continue to grow in her faith while I was gone. I *knew* she would remain close to Him. The problem is, we fail the moment we start assuming something about another person. What if her relationship hadn't been going well and she was fighting some internal battle? We never had this conversation, so frankly, I had no idea.

Something I have learned more recently, years after Everest, is that everything is hard to do in solitude. Pursuing your faith . . . achieving your dreams . . . It doesn't matter what you're trying to do. You need that cornerman by your side. Without him, or in my case, her, there is a pretty good chance you're either going to be miserable or fail.

## RACHEL

The day had finally come. We'd survived Everest and made it through attempt number one of Ranger School. Now I would finally find out if my husband would be coming home to me for good! I was in church that morning when my phone went straight to voice mail. What is up with my phone not ringing during incredibly important moments? I speed-walked out of the church, without causing a major scene, and listened to my voice mail from Harold.

"Right when I'm calling to tell you that I'm coming home to see you, you don't answer . . . so . . . ummm. This is your husband, and I will be seeing you in three days! I got a GO [Ranger School lingo for passing]! And I love you so much! And I can't wait! I'm so excited to finally see you! So, I'm gonna call you later today, uh, so try to keep your phone on you if you can. But I am coming home to see you for good, so I can't wait to be in your arms and to kiss you and to hold you. I love you so much!"

# The Next Adventure

**RACHEL**

After nearly a year of feeling like I was always holding my breath, I finally had the security I'd been so desperate for. I allowed a flood of emotions to pour out as I finally let go of holding it all together. I collapsed into the comfort of having Harold home again, no longer fearing for his life at every moment or waiting for the phone to ring with bad news. On top of that, I had formed a community of people through YouTube who cared about my life, who had watched my highs and lows through the 463 videos I had uploaded. We call them our Earls Fam because that's what they've become to us: family.

Now that there was more stability in our lives, I was more eager than ever for our family to grow. Since I hadn't gotten pregnant before Everest or Ranger School, I started to question if I would be able to get pregnant at all. I was painfully aware of how many couples struggle to conceive, and the what-ifs were often in my thoughts: *What if something is wrong? What if this never happens for us?* I pushed these thoughts to the back of my mind and instead blamed all those not-pregnant tests on bad timing.

By November, I wasn't the only one anxious about when we would get pregnant. Everyone knew we had been trying since February. Earlier in the year, I'd sent my brother a letter in the mail, and after opening it, he texted me to tell me how excited he got when he saw it. He could have sworn it was a pregnancy announcement. It wasn't.

We took Harold's mom and sister out to dinner one night, and after we finished eating and got in the car, they both looked at us and laughed because the whole time we were eating, they were expecting us to tell them "the big news" at any moment. Unfortunately, it just wasn't happening for us.

I had been tracking everything like a hawk, and right before Thanksgiving, I was two days late. Since Harold and I were actively trying to get pregnant, we talked about every little detail related to it and the timing. This made it significantly harder to hide if I was pregnant, and I wanted to surprise him in a special way.

## HAROLD

I had no idea how hard it was to get pregnant before this. We went all-out Army mission on this thing. We had a calendar tracking our best windows of opportunity for the month. And I was watching Rachel for any sign or symptom that our mission was successful. Anytime she made a comment about her stomach hurting, I thought, *She must be pregnant!* Only ate one brownie instead of three? *Food aversion: she must be pregnant.* Ate five brownies instead of three? *Eating for two: a dead giveaway!* That's odd—she seems to be sitting on the couch a little more than yesterday. *Clearly fatigue. Yep, done deal! She's gotta be preggers.*

## RACHEL

I wasn't at all surprised when Harold noticed the timing and straight up asked me if I was pregnant. I had so much hope that I was finally pregnant, since by now Harold's body had recovered from Ranger

School and Everest. I thought for sure his hormones would be back to normal and that our timing had been perfect. So I lied. I put on my best acting performance and told him I wasn't pregnant. I still hadn't taken a pregnancy test because I didn't want to take it too early and disappoint myself, but I was pretty sure it was finally our time.

I woke up on Thanksgiving morning anxious but so excited. I pulled out a test, did my business, and waited three minutes. And there it was: one single pink line. I wasn't pregnant. Ah, that moment sucked. I didn't understand, and I felt so discouraged. I imagined that moment so differently. I had even thought about how perfect the timing was because we would be with both our families on Thanksgiving and could tell them in person. That was a really hard day.

As if the past year hadn't been stressful enough, Harold received orders that we would be heading to Fort Stewart, Georgia, in a few months and that the unit he would be joining, 1-30th Infantry, was scheduled to deploy that August. The news of Harold's pending deployment was like a left hook jab out of nowhere. We were finally standing on two feet again and BAM! Life was throwing us right back down. I had already lived through so many fears about getting pregnant back when Harold was leaving for Everest, and now I was adding even more to the list.

*What if we don't get pregnant before he leaves?*

Then it would be at least three years from when we started trying, and that's assuming we get pregnant soon after he returns.

*What if we do get pregnant and he misses the birth? Do I really want to go through that alone?*

Month after month with no pregnancy was crushing my spirits. All I could think was, *When will the timing ever be right?* It was obvious that things were not working out according to my timeline, but all I could really do was trust that God's timing was better than mine. Nothing would stop us from the one thing we wanted more than anything: growing our family. It was just a matter of how and when, and for those answers we turned to God for clarity and peace.

We had already learned that in the darkest and most difficult times, God is still there.

Remember how Harold was sure God had this grand plan for him to meet his wife in some crazy way? Well, naturally, he felt the same way about us getting pregnant. This time, he had it in his mind that I would be pregnant by Christmas.

I had seen my fair share of negative tests by the holiday season. I knew all too well the lingering empty feelings after a negative test. Taking a pregnancy test for the first time when you're trying to get pregnant is exciting. Taking a pregnancy test when you've seen the same negative result over and over is terrifying and anxiety ridden. The last thing I wanted was for anything to take away my joy on Christmas, especially after having such a blue Thanksgiving.

I decided I wasn't going to take a test, but on Christmas Eve, I had a change of heart. I was in full disbelief seeing that second pink line for the first time. After many prayers of thanksgiving, several hours of planning, and four positive pregnancy tests later, I was ready to give Harold the best Christmas he had ever had. Of course, I decided to film everything. This moment not only changed our family forever but also launched my YouTube channel to new heights as our pregnancy announcement video went viral.

## HAROLD

There was no doubt in my mind she was pregnant. I mean, I was still pretty sure she had been pregnant for a while and was just waiting to tell me on Christmas. By this point, we'd also had a lot of practice making a baby together, which had to have helped our chances in some way.

Rachel woke me up at six on Christmas morning, wide awake, and we took turns opening presents. With each one, my mind was racing.

*Maybe this is it . . . Shoot, just a pair of socks.*

"Aw, thanks, hunny, for the socks."

I picked up another present. *Oh man, this present is oddly shaped. I bet this is how she's going to tell me . . . Nope, just a mug.*

When I opened the last present, I started to get down. I was bummed. Then she said she had one more present she wanted to give me.

*Praise Jesus, hallelujah, this it! This is it! This is it!*

Turns out it was a present from her parents. A computer monitor.

We got up off the floor and gave our puppies their presents, and then she walked closer to me. Hugging me and looking into my eyes with a sweet smile, Rachel spoke in her cute voice she uses only with me.

"I think there might be one more gift for you."

She gave me a kiss, said she hadn't wrapped it, pulled my Santa hat down over my eyes, then walked me back into our room to wait for a few minutes. She came back and grabbed my hand, leading me back into the family room. I made some stupid comments asking if it was a new couch or maybe a La-Z-Boy, trying not to get my hopes up again. But then I heard our wedding song playing, and I knew something was up. My heart started racing.

I pulled the Santa hat back up to uncover my eyes and looked down to see a small baby onesie with a note that said "Merry Christmas, DAD!" I immediately threw my arms around Rachel, my voice and body shaking. "Hunny! I'm gonna be a dad? I'm gonna be a dad! I love you! Are you serious?" After a challenging year of hardships, growth, and being worlds apart, the day we had dreamed about, prayed about, and been trying for had finally come.

WE WERE PREGGERS!!!*

---

* Watch our pregnancy announcement at Earls.org/baby.

# Epilogue

## RACHEL

On September 8, 2017, we welcomed baby Leo into the world. My pregnancy turned out to be a mountain of its own, as I endured unusual chronic back pain. Everyday things such as sitting, standing, and driving would often leave me in tears.

After giving birth, I learned I have degenerative disc disease. Though my pregnancy was one of the hardest seasons I've been through, I felt closer to understanding Jesus's sacrificial love than I ever had before.

Having both my husband and my son is a blessing I'll never take for granted. I finally have the family I'd always prayed for. Parenting is another trek into the unknown, full of triumphs and fears, but that's a whole other adventure (or book!).

Our pregnancy announcement video ended up going viral and was viewed more than six million times on YouTube, fifty-one million times on Facebook, and fourteen million times on China's social platforms. It was even featured on DailyMail.com. The love and excitement between us was quite literally felt around the world. From there, my YouTube channel took off. I now have over half a million people who follow our life journey.

In 2018, we started the Earls Family Foundation to give back to our online community, hoping to make a deep and tangible difference in our followers' lives. This had been a goal of mine from the very beginning, and once I shared it with Harold, he was all in!

We have an amazing volunteer staff, led by Harold's sister, Liz, who all have a passion for serving others. With their invaluable support, in our very first year we were able to give back over $20,000 to our community through twenty-seven different projects, blessing nearly thirty families. Projects ranged from giving Christmas presents, covering the cost of a service uniform, providing a washing machine to a family in need, awarding scholarships for higher education, and so much more!*

We've moved four times in four years. Harold served as an airborne Ranger–qualified light infantry platoon leader and was then selected to lead a battalion's scout and sniper platoon at Fort Stewart, Georgia. He was next promoted to captain, and we are currently living in Washington, DC, where he serves as the Commander of the Guard of Honor at the Tomb of the Unknown Soldier in Arlington National Cemetery. He absolutely loves his job and tells me just how much every day when he comes home.

Harold has always been about challenging himself, and being the commander at the Tomb of the Unknown Soldier has certainly provided that opportunity. The guards are tasked by Congress to maintain the highest standards and traditions of the United States Army and of our nation, all while keeping a constant vigil guarding our country's most hallowed ground. His job makes for some early mornings and long evenings, but we continue to make the most of the time we do have together. It is inspiring to see the deep love he has for our country and his Soldiers, and I am always so proud of him.

* Check out Earlsfam.org to see more.

I gave birth to our second son, Wyatt, on May 23, 2019. I still struggle with back issues, but there's nothing I wouldn't do for our children. Between the four of us and our two dogs, our home is always a little crazy and a lot of fun! I can't say it's easy, but these truly are the best years of my life. We are already making plans for baby number three, fingers crossed and God willing! Harold wants twins, but I told him my body can't handle that!

We're not sure what our next adventure will be, but we do know we're in it together. If we can survive Everest and come out stronger, with greater faith and fiercer love, then we can do anything.

# Acknowledgments

Many people throughout the years have helped us get to where we are today. There aren't enough pages to name every person and contribution, but we wanted to publicly thank a few who have made it possible.

## HAROLD

Connor Love, without your help, none of this would have happened. To say "thank you" hardly suffices for the amount of work you put in. You dedicated hundreds, if not thousands, of hours to selflessly help the cause. Your leadership and ability to solve problems were instrumental; I felt like we were constantly running into obstacles, but your resolve enabled us to keep knocking them down. I am so thankful to consider you one of my closest friends. Thanks so much for believing in me, our team, and our mission.

CSM Burnett, there is no one I look up to more than you. I respect how you lead and love your family, and I strive to emulate that. You have always "cared that much" and have left a lasting impression on me. Thank you for cofounding USX and for your involvement in helping veterans across the country.

Tommy, you have always been my best friend and someone I've

looked up to from the moment we met on the West Forsyth base-ball field. You have been there for me on my best days and on my worst. Thanks for heeding the call and stepping into the challeng-ing role of Base Camp manager. Without your hard work sending late-night emails, carrying heavy communication gear, and so on, our awareness campaign for PTSD would not have been the success it was. I love you, partner, and I look forward to many more decades of friendship as we raise our families together.

Melissa Thomas, you believed in me from the very beginning. I'll never forget our first phone call when you shared about MAJ Thomas and expressed your willingness to help support us in any way, saying, "I know this is something Chris would have loved to do." I am so thankful that over the years we have developed the friendship we have today.

Dave, you are knowledgeable, experienced, and a joy to be around. I am so impressed by your intellect and ability to think crit-ically and solve problems. The only way any media footage made it back home was because you captured it and found ways to send it. Undoubtedly, we were able to reach the many veterans we did because of your role.

Chad, my man! You are inspiring. I still have distinct memories of being absolutely dog tired on the mountain and looking up to see you trucking along, carrying on a conversation with a smile on your face. I love your enthusiasm for life and your easygoing personality.

Amy Summers, what a blessing you were in raising awareness for our cause! I appreciate how open and honest you were with me. You never sugarcoated things, and I love that about you. I know we certainly didn't pay you as much as you deserved, but you went above and beyond to help us touch others.

CPT Matt Hickey, I would have loved more than anything to have you standing beside me on the summit, but fate had other plans. You were the first person, outside of Rachel, to believe in me, even when I had zero climbing experience. We formed USX together and worked relentlessly to make this dream a reality. I greatly appreciate your mentorship and guidance along the way.

An Doja, I was grateful to have such a seasoned climber and friend by my side. Thank you for believing in me and helping me accomplish my dream. I wish you and your family the best. Here's to many more successful summits.

Rachel Kirby, you stepped in at an absolutely critical and tough time to run social media for USX. I was so grateful to have your help in raising awareness and keeping families up to date with our progress on the mountain. Love you, cuz.

Em, your drive and determination from the very beginning blew me away. I'll never forget connecting with you after that *Army Times* article and knowing immediately that you were the right fit. You were an integral addition, and I am grateful to have such a stud on our team.

## RACHEL

Mom, thank you for showing up for us in the lonely hours of both Everest and the book-writing process. You truly championed us by posting thorough Facebook updates that garnered quite the following and by stepping in to communicate with family members when I was unable. You helped with book edits when I was preparing to give birth to Wyatt, and you watched the boys on several occasions so I could write. Your support has meant the world to me.

Morgan, thank you for your constant friendship and for cheering me on through every new dream of mine. You've supported my YouTube dream from the very beginning and lifted me up during my low moments. I will always remember that. I aspire to be the kind of friend you are.

## BOTH OF US

To our children: Mom and Dad love you so much—more than you'll ever know. One day when you can read this, we want you to know that we will always support your dreams and passions and encourage you to seek out experiences that help you grow as people and in your faith. Embrace your inner creativity and imagination. Pursue what you love, and chances are you'll find joy and purpose along the way.

To our immediate and extended families: thank you for your constant love and support as we embarked on a dangerous and crazy journey at a time when we were still trying to figure out how to live on our own as newlyweds. We realize we may have caused many sleepless nights for you, especially around the time of the summit push, but know that individually and together, we have grown into better people as a result. Thanks for enabling us to pursue our dreams!

To our Earls Fam community: we love you and consider you an extension of our family! Thank you for being there to talk with, cry with, and share our life with. Blessings to each and every one of you!

Bryan Norman, there are few people in this world we trust as much as you. We can't thank you enough for your dedication to helping make this happen. You were the one who got this thing off the ground, and we know we're where we are now because of you. Thanks for your friendship, mentorship, and guidance along the way. We look forward to many more years together. May God continue to bless you and your family.

Travis Thrasher, God sent you at literally the perfect time. We had hit many roadblocks with the book and were really discouraged. Your timeliness and ability to creatively restructure and edit the book turned it into something special. We are so grateful you came alongside us and brought the story to life. Thank you!

Becky Nesbitt, you are such a kind, caring, and make-it-happen kind of person. We are thankful to have you in our lives and thankful for your help in shaping the story the way you did. Your calming demeanor guided the way to turn the story into something we're really proud of. We love your hands-on approach and authenticity in caring about our story. We hope to work with you again in the future!

Karen Robison, you are such a blessing in our lives! You selflessly dedicated dozens of hours to help bring the book home. Your editing skills were invaluable and shaped our story in a meaningful way. Thank you for your encouragement and for being such a positive addition to our team.

To the WaterBrook and Penguin Random House publishing team: thank you for believing in our story and allowing us to influence others through this platform you have given us. We are forever grateful.

Susy, thanks for putting in the time to help bring our book to life. We enjoyed our many phone calls as we laughed together and shared stories. Blessings to you, and best of luck going forward.

Katie Robinson, you are gifted in capturing emotion through the lens of a camera, even in the cold December air. Our book cover would not be the same without you.

Veterans and families, this country is indebted to the sacrifice you have bestowed on this land we love. We thank all our past and present service members and their families. Service is a lifelong commitment, and many of the sacrifices you made left lasting wounds that you are still dealing with today. Know that we love you, appreciate you, and are praying for you daily. May God continue to bless you, your families, and the great US of A.

Special thanks to the companies and individual sponsors who supported the USX Everest expedition: Tony Farwell, Marc Van Buskirk, Staffan Encrantz, Mr. Urban, Toni Guzzi, Nick Farwell, the entire GovX team, Sebastian Junger, Nick Curry, Summit Climb, Colin Dunlap, Nick Anthony, Bryant Skarda, Jason Reid, Anesti Vega, Benji Marquez, MG. Medvigy, the entire USX team, Harold's Army commanders, Zac Brown and Southern Ground.